CHANGING
Lanes

Using Sports As A Vehicle to
Drive Success
On & Off The Court

ASHLEY ROBERTS

www.selfpublishn30days.com

Published by *Self Publish -N- 30 Days*

Printed in the United States of America

ISBN: 978-1798123676

1. Student Athletes 2. Self Help 3. Inspiring Memoir

Ashley Roberts: Competitive Edge, LLC.

Changing Lanes

Disclaimer/Warning:

This book is intended for lecture and entertainment purposes only. The author or publisher does not guarantee that anyone following these steps will be successful in life. The author and publisher shall have neither liability responsibility to anyone with respect to any loss or damage cause, or alleged to be caused, directly or indirectly by the information contained in this book.

ACKNOWLEDGMENTS

Without the support and love from everyone, this book would not have been possible. Writing a book has always been a dream and with your help and encouraging words it was able to become a reality.

To Natalie England: First and foremost, thank you! All of the late nights back and forth on book ideas and being on the phone listening to me vent is what got me through this process. To think that we met a few months ago when writing a book was just a thought to being there every step of the way until the book was completely finished. I cannot thank you enough for your patience, dedication and determination in making sure I wrote this book. You are truly one of a kind. If you don't have a Natalie England, get yourself one!

To AJ Abrams, Amber Quist, Cat Osterman, Mark Henry, Ricky Brown, Karen Aston, Jean-Paul Hebert, Krystal Ellis, Keeley Hagen, Cathy Self Morgan and Jill Sterkel: Thank you for taking time out of your busy schedules to be a part of this book. Without you, readers wouldn't be able to get valuable information to help them grow as athletes. This process was much harder than expected, as some interviews had to be re-done, but each of you were very patient in the process and willing to help in any way possible.

To Tina Kein: If it wasn't for you, I am not sure I would have been prepared for any of the jobs I have gotten. Thank you for staying on me and being right there when I needed you, whether that was to fix my resume, to help me with my master's or to seek any advice. They say once you graduate everyone moves on to the next ones coming up.

That was and is not the case with Tina. Anything I need, I can call on her right away!

To my friends: Thank you for being who you are! Sweet, kind, honest, and supportive friends. From helping me stay focused to going through 444 pictures to pick the perfect one, to helping me narrow down a title, it was much appreciated and did not go unnoticed.

To my family who always catches the short-end of the stick: Without you, I would have messed up on lots of the stories in the book, ha ha. Thanks for being a listening ear and helping out whenever you could to ensure this book was a success! Thank you for always speaking positively into my life even when I was not in the mood to hear it at times. Thank you for being the support system I needed to get through this process.

To my coaches who took a chance on me: This book came to fruition because of you, because you granted me the opportunity to go through life playing basketball. You allowed me to have a platform through the game of basketball that I can continue to use to impact other athletes like myself.

Having an idea and bringing it to life through a book would not have been possible without Self Publish -N- 30 Days as well as everyone mentioned above. A very special thank you to my editor, Cindy, who was one of a kind. She simply listened and executed. Experiences, setbacks and accomplishments brought this book to life. Thanks again.

TABLE OF
CONTENTS

Foreword 1

Introduction 3

PART ONE - PRE-SEASON 11

Chapter 1   Health is Wealth 13

Chapter 2   I Don't Want Any Problems 23

Chapter 3   No Pass, No Play 31

Chapter 4   Pressure Busts Pipes 41

Chapter 5   Going on a Ride 49

PART TWO - IN SEASON 59

Chapter 6   Where Did Time Go? 61

Chapter 7   Make it Happen 69

Chapter 8   Let's Play the Talking Game 77

Chapter 9   It Takes More Than YOU 87

Chapter 10 Prepare to Win or Prepare to Lose 95

PART THREE - POST/OFF SEASON 101

Chapter 11 Interviews With Athletes 103

Chapter 12 Interviews With Coaches 157

Chapter 13 Interview With Athlete & Retired Coach 191

Conclusion 199

FOREWORD

Life after sports has always been one of my favorite topics. So, I was excited to see that Ashley was tackling a subject that has the potential to engage and empower athletes, coaches and parents all around the world. In my 37 years as head coach at the University of Texas at Austin, I was fortunate to coach many outstanding young women. I always believed that my job was more than coach, that my role in and of itself was bigger than basketball. That's the focus of *Changing Lanes*. Ashley adeptly shares how to use the lessons learned through sports as a foundation for building a successful life outside of sports.

What do I do when my athletic career ends? That's the question facing every athlete, regardless of their age, gender, sport or participation level. It's never been an easy question to answer, primarily because most athletes have difficulty imagining their lives without active sports participation. But that day will come. It comes for all of us — even coaches. So, how do you prepare for that last jump shot that last putt, that last 200 meters or that last touchdown?

Ashley does a great job of not only prepping young athletes for the end of their careers, but she also offers insights to how they can leverage the many skills and relationships they've developed along the way. I watched Ashley play basketball at The University of Texas, and what I remember most, aside from her competitive nature, is that she was a great teammate. Always cheering when she wasn't in the game. Always leading by example when she was on the floor. Those traits are hard to miss in a sport as public as basketball. Those traits transfer well to the "real world".

Perhaps what struck me most about Ashley were the moves she started making immediately after graduation. She started her own basketball company. She became a real estate agent. She started speaking to and empowering young girls around Austin. As I read *Changing Lanes,* it became apparent to me that Ashley clearly understands the concept of reaching back and giving back, and I know that every athlete or parent will see the tremendous value on every page of this playbook for success after sports.

Jody Conradt

Naismith Hall of Fame Women's Basketball Coach

Former Women's Basketball Coach/Women's AD

The University of Texas

Introduction

"Have a great day at school and keep your bags close to you. I love you." My mom would say this to me every morning before dropping me off at school. Ring. Ring. Those bells would go off for school to get started and here I would be walking down the halls with two bags bigger than me on my shoulders. "How much for the gum?" "Twenty-five cents for a stick." "I will take four." And the kid would hand me $1. I would make $1 off a twenty-five cent pack of gum!

Yes, I was the candy girl selling to all the kids in school. I was in the third grade. One stick of gum, fruities, chewies and lollipops were twenty-five cents. If you do not know what fruities and chewies are, please stop reading this book for a second and go look it up and order yourself some! Flamin' Hot Cheetos and Capri Suns were fifty cents. Starburst and Skittles were $1. Oh, let's not forget honey buns. They were a whopping $2!

My goal was to get at least $5 from my customers. Most orders were two bags of Flamin' Hot Cheetos, a Capri Sun, and a honey bun. Or, they bought all that with only one bag of the Hot Cheetos. Some would even spend $5 just on fruities and chewies. Either way, my goal was to get them to see my products (my candy) and upsell them for more! Here's how it went:

Kid: *"Can I get a bag of Hot Cheetos?"*

Me: *"Would you like a drink to go with those Hot Cheetos?"*

Kid: *"Yeah, I'll take that."*

Me: *"How about something sweet to go with that? Maybe some candy or a honey bun?"*

Kid: *"Give me a honey bun."*

Me: *"You are going to be wanting something later on and I may not be around."*

Kid: *"You're right. Go ahead and give me two fruities and two chewies."*

Me: *"Here you go!" And, I am thinking in my head, "Bam, I did it!"*

With a little conversation, that order went from $1 to $5 real quick. All I did was ask questions and help my customer see the value in more items. My goal was to do that with each customer. Some wanted just what they asked for, but a majority almost always got more. They knew what they wanted and they wanted more. Even better, they would send other customers my way or find a way to find me during the school day later on. I would glance at the door while in class and see students waving through the door for me to come out because they wanted to purchase something.

"Ms. (whoever the teacher was), may I go to the restroom, please?" I would ask.

"Yes, of course you can," the teacher would answer.

I would get up with my bag and hobble right out the door.

"Why do you need your bag?" the teacher would always ask.

My answer remained the same at all times, "I don't trust anyone around my belongings."

I would walk right out. The teacher would give this puzzled look, probably trying to figure out how I knew such a big word at a young age. I would make my sales and head right back to the classroom just in time for the lesson.

Another one of my goals was to have half of my products sold by lunchtime and close to sold out after lunchtime. I wanted to be sold out right after school and restock that night for the next morning. That goal was met more times than not! My target audiences were the kids in my class, since I saw them more than anyone else. I also used them to market my business for me. I spent $0 on marketing, as they would spread the word for me and bring me new customers who would purchase and go tell the other kids. It was a repeating process and very successful.

Our school consisted of Pre-K through sixth grade students and I was the only one selling candy at the time. Imagine the ROI I was getting. After the kids saw that I was doing a good job selling candy, some of them tried to do the same thing. They sold the same exact products I sold, but they were not seeing the same success I was.

That moment, in the third grade, I realized that relationships and building connections were important. How can someone do the same thing I am doing, but not get the same results I am getting? It was simple. I was not selling candy to the kids. I was selling a good experience. I was friendly. I talked to them and made them feel welcomed! They left with not only products, but with a smile on their face. This built a connection and built loyal customers. Others could sell the same thing I sold, but they couldn't interact with customers the way I did. That was the difference.

You know that store that all the kids hang out at after school or that one that is considered the "neighborhood store" since you can walk right to it? That was Rainbow Deli. Rainbow Deli was my go to place and my mom would make sure I was there each time inventory was running low. I believe she thought that since she was taking me to the Deli that she could get things for free, but she was sadly mistaken.

My family would ask for free things, and I would always make them pay for it. This was my business and my business meant everyone paid! Sometimes, that meant that I had to sleep with my bags in my bed with me so they wouldn't sneak in and get anything. Safe to say, my entrepreneurship journey started a bit early.

What do you want to do for the rest of your life? Play (insert sport here) says every athlete. Well, at least, that was my response. As good as it sounds, the chances of that actually happening are very slim. Less than two percent to be exact, with women's basketball being even less. But, don't worry. I've got you covered with *Changing Lanes*.

This book will help any athlete to not only remember the amazing skills and talents they have, but also to see the possibilities of life in front of them, whether they have retired from sport or plan to do so (as everyone will at some point.)

If you are looking for advice on how to use sports for your benefit from someone who has been through the process, *Changing Lanes* is for you. I have "been there, done that" and can help you leverage sports to your benefit. My goal is to train, inspire and educate you to reach and succeed at your next level using sports. Whatever that next level is. Could it be a doctor? How about a teacher? What about a coach? Or even a lawyer. The choice is yours.

With over 20 years of experience in the sports world as an athlete and years of experience as a coach, I have the answers you are looking for, and if I don't, some of the notable people in the book will. Basketball has been in my life since I was a toddler and it has taken me to some amazing places, allowed me to meet some amazing people and granted me the opportunity to do some amazing things.

Throughout the journey, it did beat me up with two surgeries; one being a torn ACL and the other being microfracture surgery. I broke my pinky. It still looks crazy and does not straighten. It took some wear and tear on my body. However, it was worth it and I think it is safe to say I used it to my benefit. We will get into how I have continued to leverage sports to my benefit throughout the book, but for now, let's focus on why YOU need this book!

Figuring out what to do with yourself when sports are over can be a difficult task to look at. This may be why many athletes try to avoid it and wait until the problem occurs. Although you do not want to take the fun from your sport and you want to live in the moment of playing, you need to be prepared for when the time comes.

Throughout this book, I will reveal principles you should be aware of that will help you be successful in life after sports. I will share some of my stories and how these principles have helped me transition from student-athlete to entrepreneur. By reading this book, you will be a step ahead of the game and will have a better understanding of how sports can truly be an advantage to you.

My hope is that you will be able to take away some key things that will help you use sports as a vehicle to drive success on and off the court. Before we dive into the book, I would like to tell you about this terrible disease that some athletes encounter when they finally hang up the shoes. If not proactive, this disease can spread very quickly and can become deadly. It will be deadly to your passion, dreams and love for life. However, unlike many diseases, this one cannot be treated with a doctor's care. Hopefully I am catching some of you before getting this disease and if you have already caught it, no worries. If you apply the principles from this book, you will be cured and disease free!

Now, I am sure you are very worried and wondering what kind of crazy disease is this. This disease is FTA, and no, it's not free throw attempts. It is called First Thing Available. Many athletes jump to the first thing available after sports and get stuck in that same spot for years and years. At least I did anyway (but only for a little bit). Developing FTA causes depression, and if not careful, can cause you to become very miserable.

After hearing such bad news, I do have some good news! If you are currently in a good spot in life and enjoying what you are doing, then you do not suffer from FTA. Congratulations! If you are not where you want to be, are you doing what you need to do to get where you want to go? If not, it's okay! Are you that athlete who has no idea what they will do when they are done playing? How about the one who thinks they are not credible because they have only played sports and don't have experience in the job world? Or what about the one who doesn't understand the important qualities learned through sports?

Changing Lanes is here to help you avoid severe FTA. If you are in the beginning stages of it, we can get it under control. Let's get a hold of it before you reach the final stages of FTA that is deadly. Deadly to your passion, dreams and love for life. Lets go to work! See you inside.

Part One

PRE-SEASON

WHAT YOU NEED TO KNOW AND WHY

In this section, I will talk about five important reasons sports are critical for your development.

Chapter 1

HEALTH IS WEALTH

"Sport is a preserver of health."
- Hippocrates

One of the main reasons sports are important is that it helps you stay healthy and active. It is imperative to exercise daily and I can tell you non-athletes will not do this or at least will not be consistent with it. Being an athlete allows you to exercise while doing something you enjoy. That's a win-win situation. I am not the health connoisseur, but I do know exercise plays a vital part in your conditions to be healthy. I am almost willing to bet if I did not play sports, I would not have taken time out to exercise regularly. And for you former athletes, I know you are nodding your head, agreeing as well.

For one, I hate running! How is that possible? You run while playing basketball. There is a big difference. I can run up and down the court with no problems, but running just for the sake of it is a no-no for me. I can't tell you how many times my coach "suggested" we do cross country, and I respectively declined every single time. :) My coach telling us we are going outside to run a mile was like her telling me to go tryout for volleyball. Lord knows, that would be an embarrassment waiting to happen. Yes, it was that extreme to me. However, those

Friday mile runs were key to me being in shape and it made it so much better being able to do it with my teammates. Starting it almost always seemed impossible, but finishing it was always a sign of relief and excitement that I finished.

Speaking of running a mile, please take my advice, and never eat four bags of Hot Cheetos before practice. It was my junior year of high school and we had mile Friday, just as we did every Friday before season. Two bags of Hot Cheetos and a Gatorade was my go-to at school. But on this particular Friday, I was craving Hot Cheetos and bought four bags and ate them all right before practice.

We got dressed to head outside and there went my stomach, bubbling, twisting and turning. I turn around and went to the restroom. By the time I was able to come out, the team had finished stretching and listening to coach's 10-minute speech that she gave before we ran. They were already running. I started stretching, and there it went again. Eventually, I was able to start running and finish my mile run. Lesson learned. I never ate four bags of Hot Cheetos again!

Statistics from nhs.uk/live-well show that people who do regular physical activity have up to a:

➤ 35% lower risk of coronary heart disease and stroke

➤ 50% lower risk of type 2 diabetes

➤ 50% lower risk of colon cancer

➤ 20% lower risk of breast cancer

➤ 30% lower risk of early death

➤ 83% lower risk of osteoarthritis

➤ 68% lower risk of hip fracture

➤ 30% lower risk of falls (among older adults)

➤ 30% lower risk of depression

➤ 30% lower risk of dementia

Looking at these stats makes me want to stop writing for a bit and find a gym!

Being healthy is not only about exercise. What you feed your body and how much sleep you are getting plays a huge role as well. In high school, I ate whatever I wanted, and it did not have any affect on my play on the court. Sometimes, I did not eat at all. Yeah, I have this weird thing of not eating sometimes. I went to sleep at whatever time I wanted (if my parents didn't come check on me), and it didn't affect my play on the court. As I got older, that changed.

When I got to college, I had to eat first just to have enough energy for practice. Eating three times a day was a minimum, but it was recommended to eat three times a day and have two snacks. A typical day for me was pancakes and eggs for breakfast. Boy, I sure do miss those pancakes at San Jacinto. The lady in the back always made my pancakes to perfection. A little brown around the edges, but not too crispy. The pancake had that golden color and was sooo fluffy! My snack was normally an apple or a banana with peanut butter. I can only eat bananas with peanut butter. Otherwise, bananas are nasty!

My typical lunch was either chicken quesadillas or a salad. My salad was lettuce, chicken, eggs and if I wanted to be really healthy, I would sometimes throw some tomatoes and cucumbers in it. The only way I could eat them was if they were cut up really small to where I could barely taste it. My other snack was usually either yogurt with granola in it or a granola bar. Dinner was normally baked chicken with mashed potatoes, corn and a roll. Dinner would get tricky sometimes, because a lot of times I would use that as a cheat meal and head to Wingstop to get my 8-piece original hot combo with extra seasoning on the fries and eat it with their ranch.

As I began to get into the routine of eating, and eating the right things for the most part, I was able to see a big difference in my energy level at practice and in games. Water intake was crucial, but that wasn't a problem, as we had to drink at least four bottles a day. Between the huge water bottle we had to carry around throughout the day and the water bottles that were never empty at practice, I was drinking more than four bottles a day.

Now let's talk about sleep. It was all or nothing with me. I was either never sleeping or always sleeping. There was no balance for me.

A friend would ask, "Want to go to the mall?"

"Naw, I am going home to take a nap," I would answer.

She would ask, "Want to go bowling?"

"Naw, I am about to go take a nap," I would answer.

That seemed to be my response to most questions. There were times we would get back very late from games and I would still have to wake up early for class. I took advantage of any gaps in-between my schedule and went to sleep! Sleep was in someone's room, outside of class as I waited for it to get started or in the locker room. The best sleep was the five-minute naps while on the bus, going to practice, or to another class. For some reason, the short naps were always the best.

In my opinion, in terms of when you are done with your sport, the older you get, the harder it is for you to exercise. This is a problem I have encountered personally with myself. Once I finished playing college ball, my exercise routine became inconsistent. In the midst of that, I lost focus of my overall health and was diagnosed with a condition called Ulcerative Colitis. UC is an inflammatory bowel disease that mainly affects the lining of the large intestine. Pain after pain, hospital visit after hospital visit, doctor bill after doctor bill (those don't stop coming), I have had to endure this terrible disease.

When I stopped working out consistently, and my stress levels rose, my stomach began to hurt. At first, I thought I was just having stomach pains, but when I started to see blood coming out of the backend, I knew something was wrong. After several attempts of me being stubborn trying to fight through everything, I finally gave in and went to see a doctor. Long story short, I was diagnosed with UC and the doctors did not have a direct answer as to how I developed it. However, they did ask me four questions.

How much water do you drink daily? How long do you exercise? On a scale of 1-10, how stressed are you? What does your diet look like? If these questions would have been asked to me as a student athlete, it would have been over four bottles a day, more than an hour and half a day, stress level would have depended on the day, ha ha, and diet would have been fairly good. Answering these questions now, I would say, "One bottle on a good day, exercise – depends on the day and how much work I have to get done. Stress? Whew – 10. Does diet still exist these days?"

These were all of the things we naturally encountered as an athlete that we don't think about as non-athletes. In reality, taking care of my body has been one of my toughest challenges, being that I have so many other things to focus on. You would think it would be easy as pie for an ex-athlete to be healthy, right? What I can say is that going through many workouts and talking to our nutritionist in college, prepared me in the facts of knowing what to eat, when to eat, and what exercises to do.

Now, it is just a matter of actually applying the information. When talking to the doctors, they expressed that playing sports had been a factor in fighting off this disease for as long as it did. The exercising and water intake were two important factors and playing sports allowed me to do that. Oddly enough, I encountered the condition after I finished collegiate sports. Coincidence, huh?

IT'S IN
YOUR COURT

➤ What is one thing that you can change in order to live a healthier lifestyle?

_____

_____

_____

_____

➤ By making this one change, how will it benefit you?

_____

_____

_____

_____

➤ What is your action plan to make this happen?

_____

_____

_____

_____

➤ When will you begin your action plan?

_____

_____

_____

_____

Example:

One thing I can do better is to workout consistently. By doing this I will see my body changing to be more fit. I will get in a routine of doing something everyday and it is good for my health overall! My action plan is to first start by working out at least three days a week. I will work myself up to working out every day after doing three days a week for a few weeks to gain some momentum and consistency. Once I have that going, I will then add an extra day and continue the process until I am working out everyday.

Notes

_____

_____

_____

_____

_____

_____

_____

_____

_____

_____

_____

Chapter 2

I DON'T WANT ANY PROBLEMS

"Growing up, if I hadn't had sports, I don't know where I'd be.
God only knows what street corners I'd have been standing on and God
only knows what I'd have been doing, but instead I played hockey and
went to school and stayed out of trouble."
- Bobby Orr

Another key reason that sports is important is that it helps you stay busy and out of trouble. As an athlete, there is not much time to focus on distractions. Yes, you are a young teenager and things will happen, but the majority of athletes are steered away from major problems. Pregnancy, crime rates and drug abuse are the main concerns for the youth. In 2015, a total of 229,715 babies were born to females aged 15–19 years, for a birth rate of 22.3 per 1,000 females in this age group. See www.cdc.gov/teenpregnancy. There were 809,700 juvenile arrests made in 2017, which ranged from murder to robbery to vandalism down to curfew violations, just to name a few. See www.ojjdp.gov/ojstatbb/crime.

Yes, you are a college athlete who wants to go to every party in sight. However, you also know you have those 6:00 am workouts the next day, or a game to prepare for the next day. There were a few times my teammates, as well as myself, tried the "We are in college, let's party all night" line and went to practice the next day very sluggish and regretting the decision. If we didn't think our coach knew that we were out late the night before, we were sadly mistaken. Never again. Never again.

Being involved in sports allows athletes to first, be busy, to not have time for those activities, and second, to think about how those situations can negatively impact the sport they are playing. It does come with consequences and most athletes are not willing to suffer the consequences of what those activities may encounter.

"You can never go out and have fun with us," said one of my middle school friends. One weekend, my friend wanted me to spend the night at her house because her parents were heading out of town. My friend was inviting two other girls over and the plan was to invite some guy friends over as well. She told me that if I didn't come, she would not be my friend anymore. Peer pressure. I did want to hang out with my friends and I did not want to lose her as a friend, but I knew if I told my parents the truth about no parents and boys being there they would say no. What did I do? Keep reading!

"Mom, Dad, Brittany is having a sleep-over and she invited me to come over," I said. "Will her parents be there?" my dad asked.

I said, "Yes, of course. Why would I ask if they weren't?"

That should have hinted that I was not telling the truth.

"You have a basketball tournament and need to focus on your game, so you cannot go," my dad said.

That's pretty much how every response from him went when I would ask to do things with my friends. However, I was glad he said that for this night. That weekend, those same guy friends that came over got into an altercation and the police were involved. This was ultimately relayed to my friend's parents, as well as all the parents of the kids there. I surely dodged that bullet and that friend. There are always those around you who do not share your drive and purpose. They are walking a different road. Beware of how easy it can be to follow the crowd or those walking that different road. It only takes one bad decision to take you where you do not want to go.

My parents, especially my dad, always pushed me to focus on my priorities. And for most of my life, the priority was basketball, and it made me put everything else in focus. The decisions I made centered on what would serve me well on the basketball court and also in life. Of course, as a kid, I thought my dad was too hard on me – I wanted to have fun! I never wanted to do anything crazy and always thought I made the smart decisions. But as I grew older, I realized he was trying to protect me from everyone else making the wrong decisions and me being in the wrong spot at the wrong time. You can't prevent everything, but you can sure control what is in your control.

When your friends are acting up in class, you know you can't join in on it because you can't afford to go to ISS (in school suspension) or get a referral. While your friend may not have any consequences, you will. At our high school, if we got a referral or sent to ISS, we could not play the very next game and we had consequences of whatever our coach decided that day. Boy, don't I remember the day I got a referral.

"You are out of dress code," my teacher said to me. "That is a referral and you will be sent to ISS for the remainder of the day." My eyes were as big as a bright light shining in my face at nighttime. "Ms. Caldwell, I left my belt at home because I was rushing. Please, can I find a belt so that I do not have to go to ISS?" I asked her. Begging and pleading with her did not work and sadly enough, I landed myself in ISS. The only referral I have ever gotten and it was because of a belt.

That belt showed up once I got home and was in my dad's hand. Didn't I (wop), tell you (wop), to put out your school clothes (wop), at night (wop). Those were the belt sounds to my bottom. Over a belt? Really, Dad? Really? I sure did learn after that to never leave my belt home again.

Being an athlete almost puts you at a different standard than everyone else. You can't get in trouble, talk back to the teacher, turn in missing assignments, or miss class, if you wanted to. Well, you could, but you would have consequences for doing so. I was never able to participate in senior skip day or any of the other activities that consisted of us skipping school. I mean not that I wanted to. :) Being an athlete helps build character and positive role models. Not that everyone is perfect, but it also teaches you to learn from your mistakes and move on.

IT'S IN
YOUR COURT

➤ Identify areas in your life that you would consider to be distractions for you.

_____

_____

_____

_____

➤ What are some distractions that you would be willing to eliminate or modify? (Being on social media too much, hanging with the wrong crowd, etc.)

_____

_____

_____

➤ What are some continual problems you face in your life?

_____

_____

_____

_____

➤ Identify actions that you can take to correct or resolve those problems.

_____

_____

_____

_____

Notes

Chapter 3

NO PASS, NO PLAY

"There are many research findings which highlighted that children dabbling with both sports and academics are better focused as discipline, concentration, and time-management learnt through sports come handy."
- Samuil Majmudar, *Co-Founder and CEO EduSports*

our siblings. Four athletes. We all had different takes on school. Growing up in our family was one who loved school and would have a hissy fit for every A not received. That was me. No matter the class, I wanted what I deserved and 99.9999 percent of the time, it was an A. In sixth grade, my teacher tried to let one pass by me. Report cards came out and I opened mine, knowing I got all A's. I had a 100 in PE, 100 in music, at least a 95 in Math, English, and whatever other class I had.

When I looked at my report card, I had a 99 in music! No way. "What is this, Ms. Johnson? There is no way I got a 99 in here," I explained to her. "Ashley, it is an A. Don't worry about it." Well, that didn't sit too well with me. "Ms. Johnson, every assignment I turned in received a 100, so how did I get a 99 in the class?" "Maybe you were late or something. I don't know," she replied. That day she thought it was over.

The next day, guess who was at her door. My mom! She was a little embarrassed to be there talking to my teacher about a 99, but she knew I would not let it go and I was determined to get a 100. "Ms. Johnson, I believe you made a mistake with Ashley's grade. She showed me all of her assignments and they are all 100's. She has attended every one of your classes and she has never been late to class."

Mom knew that, because if we were late, we had to go to the office and she checked the office before talking to the teacher. "I am so sorry for the confusion and will get the grade changed immediately," she responded. Wasn't the answer I was thinking in my head, but I was excited to get my 100.

Then there was the one who hated school. He also knew if playing sports was going to be an option, passing your classes was important. That was my older brother. Dwalyn was not a fan of school, but his goal was to play college basketball. He did just enough to pass his classes to be able to participate in sports. If he failed a test and could increase his grade by retaking it, you could forget about it.

As long as he was passing, that is all that mattered to him and it grinded my mom's gears. "Why can't you care about your grades like your sister does?" she would say to him. He wouldn't say a word, but I would get it when she wasn't around. Smarty pants, smarty pants, he would always tease me with. He would go beyond for basketball, but when it came to school, he would do just enough. He would come early and leave late just for workouts, but A's and B's were not a priority.

The baby brother was one who was really smart at a young age. As time went on, he could care less about a book, math, what time class was or anything in regard to school. Believe it or not, D'rell was actually the smartest of us all and was also involved in a program called talented and gifted (TAG).

As he got older, school became less of a priority and everything else became more of the priority. My mom storms in my room, "Ashley, Ashley, D'rell made a 100 on his TAKS test!" You may be thinking I was jealous, but I wasn't (just a little bit). "D'rell how was it?" "Easy." "Did you study?" "No." "How did you get a 100?" "I put the right answers down, duh."

Smart and good at basketball. Yep, he will be in the NBA everyone thought. He was smart and talented. I admired him because he was naturally gifted. As the baby of the family, maybe we let him get away with too much, especially after our parents separated. And he didn't apply the focus or discipline necessary to convert those gifts into real-life rewards.

"If you do not pass your classes, you do not play. It's that simple D'rell," said one of his high school coaches. You know what they say. The youngest of the siblings is always the "see it to believe it" type. That's D'rell. It's strange because my parents were very strict on grades and it was understood to us (well, to me and my older brother), that we had to keep our grades up in order to do extra activities.

That freshman year was a tough one for D'rell, as he did not pass one of his classes (I believe it was math), and he was not eligible to participate in extracurricular activities (basketball). It was not that he wasn't capable of doing the work, but more of thinking high school classes would be the same as middle school. He also could not fathom the fact that, if he really didn't make a C or above, he could not play basketball until further notice. After that, he did all he could to ensure that he passed all his classes so that he could participate in extracurricular activities.

His friends were not athletes and did not pass their classes, which is why he figured he could do the same. Sounds like my middle school friend, huh? This is another reason why sports are important. It can be an incentive and a motivation to pass your classes. D'rell knew that in order to play he had to have passing grades of a C or above. Do you know a D'rell? Are you a D'rell? You read of the minor setback he went through. Do you want to miss games because you are not passing your classes? I don't think so.

At 310 Charlotte, 2:00 pm on a summer afternoon, it was about to go down. My uncle, Dwalyn, and Jessica were outside playing basketball. "Y'all play one-on-one," Uncle Steve said. From the story I was told, it was a pretty close game and then BOOM! Jessica dunks on Dwalyn. "Game over," Uncle Steve said.

Unfortunately, the game was over too soon for Jessica. She was a talented player who did not put a priority and focus on school. My older sister was a WNBA pro in the making, but she didn't have the guidance or opportunity as her other siblings had.

With her being my half-sister, my dad tried to get her to stay with us so she would have the same opportunity. When you are young and having fun, anything contrary to that goes in one ear and out the other. She declined because there were not any buses for her to take to go where she wanted to go to do the fun things we all like to do at that age.

Jessica never played against girls. She was too good and they were too scared of her. She was always outside on the playground playing against the boys. The problem is, you need more than talent to get to the next level. A talented player, with every possibility to make it professionally, will never get there without having a dedication to school and further education.

You read of the different paths each of us took. Either you can get your grades up enough to allow you to play sports, or you can allow it to keep you stuck and regret your decisions made. I can tell you, that if Jessica had made better choices, she would be in the WNBA right now! Although she could not get school down and see the bigger picture of sports, she still was able to learn some valuable lessons from playing the game. One was to always compete and keep fighting no matter what. My big sister is a fighter and will make something out of nothing.

Although Jessica made mistakes at a young age, and it cost her free education, she has learned through those mistakes and can be that example to any young athlete reading this book. Getting your education is important if you want to further your athletic opportunity, and even more, to receive free education for it.

Dwalyn will tell you, still to this day, to do what you need to do to pass. As long as you are passing, that is all that matters, which may be the best for some of you athletes. It allowed him to continue his athletic and academic career at Texas Tech University, debt free! What he has struggled with by having that mindset is he had to do more than the average to get things he wants and deserves. He is learning to have a mindset shift. That mindset, that at times, he wished he had in high school.

I will tell you, go the extra mile! If you have a C, figure out what you can do to get it to a B. If you have a B, figure out what you can do to get it to an A. If you have an A, figure out what you can do to raise it more points. GPA matters, and the better your grades are, the more qualified you are, and the less stress you have when taking the ACT or SAT. The better your GPA, the lower score you can make on those tests. More importantly, I am just big on giving it your all no matter what. That attitude allowed me to further my athletic and academic career at The University of Texas at Austin, debt free!

D'rell is still learning right now and he had three examples to learn from. He is bumping his head as he goes along. And we all know the baby is the one who thinks they know it all and will have to learn the hard way. He will tell all high school athletes to take your schoolwork seriously, because that is as easy as it will get! He did not do that, and it is one thing he regrets. However, through many setbacks, he is continuing his athletic and academic career at Broward College looking to play at the next level afterwards.

I will say, it did help having someone like my mom staying proactive and wanting her kids to get an education. She was the one staying on us about grades, while my dad stayed on us about basketball. We went to her for help with classes, registering for tests, such as ACT and SAT, or even figuring out what needed to be done for college. She was there to prepare us for the education and dad prepared us to get basketball scholarships.

Yes, you have to pass to play, but more importantly, passing your classes shows your dedication to focus in class and understand the content given. Having knowledge and digesting the information given is something you will need and learn throughout life. Certain jobs require you to pass some type of test to be considered for the position, such as coaching and real estate. There are many tests that will come your way as you proceed to dominate life.

The question is, "Are you going to have the same mindset, in that you have to pass in order to participate, or will you fail and sit out for a while?" Instead of this "pass or fail" being related to extracurricular activities, it is now referring to the game of life. As life has gone by, I have had many different tests, such as tearing my ACL in high school, having to go a different route in college (that being junior college first), to preserving the juco life, adapting to a big time college school at The University of Texas, not getting the playing time I wanted, adjusting to the schedule and tempo of a Division I college, having surgery in my knee again, dealing with pain in my back from scoliosis, graduating college and getting my degree, being diagnosed with a nasty disease called UC, running to the bathroom, hoping I make it, saving me the embarrassment of using it on myself, need I continue?

I am still passing different tests that come my way. Everything is a test. Will you pass or will you fail? What's your choice?

IT'S IN
YOUR COURT

➤ What kind of grades do you typically get, whether at school or on the job?

_____

_____

_____

_____

➤ What changes can you make to improve your grades?

_____

_____

_____

_____

➤ What tools do you use to ensure you perform well?

_____

_____

_____

_____

➤ What help are you willing to seek from others to make necessary steps to improve?

_____

_____

_____

_____

Notes

Chapter 4

PRESSURE BUSTS PIPES – PERFORMING UNDER PRESSURE

"Everything negative - pressure, challenges - are all an opportunity for me to rise."
- Kobe Bryant

I am not going to fold. It's not in me. This is the mindset athletes tend to develop over time. Playing a sport consists of lots of pressure. Pressure from your parents, peers and fans. Playing sports can be difficult at times and the higher tier you play, the more people you have to please. At all levels, athletes feel the need to please their coaches. This forces them to play to not mess up, which in return, causes them to mess up. Do you know that coach who yells at you for every mistake or the coach who takes you out the game if you breathe wrong? Yeah, I have had a few of those myself.

In return, you are so nervous to not make a mistake because you don't want to come out the game or you want to do everything perfect. How does that typically turn out? For me, trying too hard to be perfect always resulted in a mistake anyway, and I ended up where I feared –

sitting on the bench. I realized I should just play, and if I get yanked, I get yanked. Eventually I'd go back in.

At a young age, you have to worry about pleasing your parents and loved ones. Are you that player who messes up in the game and looks in the stands at your parents? Are you that parent in the stands yelling at your kid and calling their name to look at you during the games? I can't tell you how many games I have coached where I had to sit a player on the bench for looking in the stands at their parents each time they made a mistake. Not only do I see this when coaching, but also as a spectator when I go to watch other games.

To my athletes, looking in the stands for your parents' approval could be the very reason you lose out on an athletic scholarship. If a coach feels you are not going to listen to your current coach, then what makes you think they will give you a scholarship to do the same thing?

Once you reach the collegiate level, you have the pressure of fans. If you have a bad game, trust me, they will talk about you. Why did they give her a scholarship? She should not be playing. She should transfer. Fans will say all kinds of unkind things. If you have a good game, they will love on you. You are an awesome player. We love having you on the team. You are such a joy to be around. Those same fans would say nice things when you are doing well.

It's just the nature of the game. This shows you how to have tough skin and keep pushing forward. Playing sports under pressure not only teaches you how to have tough skin, but it also shows you how to perform under pressure, both on and off the court (in my case).

"I don't want to go to the doctor, Mama," as we are pulling up to see the doctor. We get out of the car and head into the doctor's office. I injured my thumb and it was not straight anymore, so my mom figured the doctor could put it back in place. The problem was, I had my middle school district championship game that day. We are sitting in the doctor's office and I am looking around daydreaming about the game. All I can see is myself jumping up and down as the buzzer winds down for the championship.

"Ashley, you can come on back now." My mom hits me, as I did not hear them because I am celebrating our win in my head. I hop up and we head back. "Woah, what do we have here?" says the doctor. She injured her thumb during practice and has a game tonight. "Can you fix it?" says my mom. "We are going to have to put a cast on it so it can heal," the doctor responded. As I sit in the cold room waiting to talk, I finally blurt out, "Can I still play today?" He chuckled and said "Sure, if you think you can play with one hand, but I do not think that is possible." All I heard was "sure".

"Coach, the doctor put her in a cast, but said she can play if she wants," my mom tells my coach. While they are having a conversation, I am as excited as a little kid in the candy store. Here I am, daydreaming again, but this time I am thinking about how I am going to play with one hand. We arrive at the gym and it's game time! "Two lines," I said as we get in lay-up lines. Right hand lay-ups went fine, but the left side was a sight to see.

I could not dribble the ball with my left hand, so I had to dribble with my right hand on left side, which felt so weird. I had to not only do that, but also I had to shoot with one hand, and that being my right hand. I couldn't even put my left hand up to help with guidance. This was going to be very interesting, I thought.

We were about to tip off and I was a nervous wreck. What if someone hits my hand? How am I going to shoot? Dribble? Pass? All of this running through my head until I saw that first shot go in. Next, I got a steal and took it all the way to the basket. Bleep. And One! I yelled. It was on then. My adrenaline was at an all-time high. I forgot about my thumb being hurt with a cast on it. 5, 4, 3, 2, 1. Game over. Not only did I play, we got the win and I didn't come out of the game. Talk about performing under pressure. Job well done.

Freshman year. Duncanville High School. A really talented team. Well-known coach who knows what she is doing. What could have been scary for me became a challenge. My goal was to make varsity. Most thought that was impossible. Not only was I just a freshman, but the team was really good, with six of the members being seniors.

The two girls that played my position were a junior and senior. That did not stop me. I continued to work on my game every single day. I made sure my dad went to the gym with me to work extra and do the best I could. I knew making the junior varsity team would have been a good accomplishment as well, but I wanted more.

"Make sure you are on time for picture day tomorrow," Coach Self said. Picture day was going to hint at what team the players would be on because you were taking the picture with the team the coach thought you would be on. To say the least, I could not sleep that night. The next day came and it was time to take the picture. Here I am standing, waiting to see if I was going to take pictures with the freshman team, junior varsity or varsity.

Varsity is up first to take their pictures. They walk up and I stand back. "What are you doing? Get up there and stand in the middle. Yes, you. I am talking to you. Hurry up before they take the picture." I was jumping for joy inside, but I played it cool and walked up to get in the varsity picture.

When I got home, I raved and raved to my family about how I took the picture with varsity. My mom was super excited, but my dad was very nonchalant. That doesn't mean anything. It's just a picture, he would say. To me, I knew that I had a high chance of making varsity. The first official practice came about and if you guessed I was practicing with varsity, you guessed wrong.

I was practicing with the junior varsity. The good thing about it was the junior varsity would go up against the varsity and all I needed to do was prove myself. I did just that. By the time of the first game, I was officially on varsity.

Not only did I make varsity, but also I was the starting point guard at Duncanville High School, one of the most well-known and respected girls' program in the country. Freshman starting on varsity. Seniors being mean to you for no reason. Trying to lead your team while you are also trying to find your role. All while being on a new campus. Talk about pressure. Job well done, Ashley.

Playing sports sure did teach me how to perform under pressure. My competitive spirit not only allowed me to perform well on the court, but also taught me how to be successful in the classroom. I developed this competitive edge throughout playing the game of basketball with the different situations I encountered.

Pressure became non-existent in my world. Maybe jitters or butterflies, as I would get before my basketball games, but feeling pressured was something I knew all too well and it no longer affected me.

IT'S IN
YOUR COURT

➤ Who do you think is putting pressure on you to be successful?

_____

_____

_____

_____

➤ If it is someone other than yourself, what can you do to put a stop to the pressure?

_____

_____

_____

_____

➤ What are some negative or unhealthy things you do when you feel under pressure?

_____

_____

_____

_____

➤ What are some positive and healthy things you do to relieve the pressure?

_____

_____

_____

_____

Notes

Chapter 5

GOING ON A RIDE – A FULL RIDE

"Some people want it to happen, some wish it would happen, others make it happen."
- Michael Jordan

Mama or Da Da were not my first words, rather it was ball. Okay, okay, I am joking (I think). When I was able to talk and not tug, I constantly asked my dad, "When are we going to the gym?" Or, "When is your next game?" Or, "When can I play on a basketball team?" The time finally came. My brother was playing on a basketball team at the YMCA and I begged and pleaded every day to be on the team. I attended all of the practices, running around dribbling the ball, until one day the coach let me practice.

After a few practices, they asked me to be on the team! My parents agreed. I was five years old and Dwalyn was eight. I was the youngest on the team, as well as the only girl. Throughout the season, I did not play much and I don't think I cared. I just wanted to be on a team and play with my brother.

My time to shine was at the free throw line for technical fouls. At the YMCA, there was a rule that you couldn't pass this certain line to press. Each time you did, you would get a technical foul, which granted the other team an opportunity to shoot free throws. The coach always picked me and I always made them. I was the best free throw shooter on the team, so that was my job.

When I would get on the court, everyone would be so nervous and scared. All they saw was how very young and tiny I was playing against all the boys. "Why is she out there playing?" they would ask. Oh man, don't let her catch the ball. Each time I had the ball, all the parents and the fans would have these frantic looks on their faces while holding their hands together tightly hoping the boys didn't hurt me.

I was happy-go-lucky, running around on the court, having the best time of my life. I would argue that I was the only one in the gym not scared and it showed that day. I was on a fastbreak going for a lay-up and out of nowhere, BOOM! One of the boys from the other team went up to block it and knocked me right into the wall. I went crashing to the ground.

Everyone jumped up, gasping for air. My mom ran out to the court to check on her baby girl and I got up like nothing happened. I shook it off and walked to the free throw line all cool like to shoot my two free throws. You can bet your money I made both of them. This was the start of that free education I was after and didn't even know it.

Third grade comes around and I am at R.L. Thornton Elementary School. They have a girls' basketball team, but it is only for fifth and sixth graders. Yeah, I already know what you are thinking and asking me. You want to know if I tried out, right? Of course I did and I made the team!

Again, the youngest on the team, but this time, it is all girls. Not only did I make the team, but I started. The smallest one on the court with my pigtails in my hair, playing with no fear at all. You would have thought I was a fifth or sixth grader by the way I performed.

The only reason people knew I was younger was because I was still so tiny. Seemed like I was never going to grow. I'll note that my dad was 6'7 and my mom 5'10. "She's going to be a special kid," other coaches would tell my parents. She wants to go to college to play basketball (by this time I knew that).

Junior year comes around and the school season is going well until November 10th. This is the day I tore my ACL. Actually, that wasn't the day my world turned around just yet, because I didn't know I tore my ACL. I just kept trying to go back in the game. The trainer kept saying that if I could jump off both legs, I could go back in, but I couldn't.

I am sure you want to know how it happened. So, imagine someone dribbling the ball up the court with NO ONE around them. They get to the half court line, hold up a hand to call the play, take one more step and fall to the ground. Yep, that is how it happened. My coach and the team thought I caught a cramp, as I was known for catching cramps.

The fact that I was ready to go back in the game after coming out indicated I should be fine. The next day, my coach and I went to the doctor and that's when my world came crashing down. "I am so sorry, but you tore your ACL and you will not be able to play the remainder of the season," the doctor said. I cried all the way from the doctor's office to the school in my coach's car. I could not believe it.

At this time, I had a ton of schools recruiting me to go to college. Yes, you can believe that went away. They moved on to the next player. I was told it would take about nine months for me to be back playing.

I would try to do everything possible to get me on the court sooner. For example, the trainer told me that once my stitches dissolved on my knee, we could go to the next phase. Guess what I did? One by one, opening up each wound and letting the fresh air hit it, I removed the stitches myself, thinking it would push the process forward. Instead, it pushed it back. My knee became infected because I opened up the wound too soon.

I continued to do things that I thought would get me on the court sooner and it just kept putting me behind. This was a big setback and had me thinking that the dream I had as a little girl was no longer possible. But was I mistaken.

By the end of my senior year, it was time to make a decision. I had options, but not options I wanted. My goal and dream was always to play in the Big 12 and I believed I had the talent to actually make that happen. Honestly, it was to play at The University of Texas, but since they never showed any interest in me, I did not think I could go there.

I had a choice to make. I could go to a smaller Division I school or take my chances and go to a junior college with the hopes of going to the Big 12. I had a talk with my summer AAU coach (the director of the program) and he told me, "Ashmama, you need to go to a junior college. You will get into the Big 12 after that. You just need to let your knee get healthy."

It was either go to South Plains Junior College, Missouri State or South Alabama. A two-year school or a four-year school. A few months after the conversation with my AAU coach, he passed away. This guy meant a lot to me. He believed in me when nobody did. He made sure I was taken care of no matter how many new players came to the program. I decided to listen to him and go to South Plains Junior College.

While most thought that I was crazy for making that decision, I knew in my heart it was the right one and I trusted what my AAU coach told me. RIP Marques Jackson (Coach Mudd). Onto college I went. For free.

Another one of the most beneficial reasons for playing sports is the opportunity to receive a free education. I heard it all the time from my parents. I knew that if I didn't get a free scholarship, then they were not sure how I would go to college. Well, my goal was to get a scholarship, academically or athletically. I wanted the athletic scholarship, because I wanted to play basketball in college.

Sports can be one avenue to get to college debt-free, and I believe, that if possible, athletes should take full advantage of that.

There are a ton of schools across the country, whether Division I, II, III, NAIA or junior college. The National Collegiate Athletic Association (NCAA) governs about 24 different collegiate sports programs at nearly 1,300 Division I, Division II, and Division III schools throughout the United States. The NJCAA has approximately 530 member colleges participating in 15 men's and 13 women's sports.

These numbers show you that there really are plenty of opportunities to receive free education through sports if you want to. Take it from me. I went to a junior college first, and if you keep reading, you will find out where I finished.

In order to get to the place where a college coach might want you to join their program, you must first take care of all of the other reasons that brought you to that place. All of the money that my parents spent over the years for my AAU teams, and any other related expenses for basketball, did not compare to how much money they would have had to spend on college.

Well, in their words, I would not have been able to go to college. If you ask either of them, they would tell you it was definitely worth every penny to invest in AAU, attend tournaments and sacrifice some things in their lives to make sure I was able to participate in sports.

All that I needed to move ahead was to attend freshman year at a junior college. I was Western Junior College Athletic Conference All Conference first team honoree, team MVP and offensive team MVP. By the end of the season, I had the option to attend University of North Texas. However, I decided not to and I came back for another year at South Plains.

Most people thought I was crazy. Just like they thought I was crazy when I chose a two-year school over a four-year school. I came back and was able to rack up the same awards, as well as All Region 5 and WBCA Honorable Mention All American team. By the end of that season, I had the option to go to University of Arkansas or Wichita State. I actually committed to go to Arkansas. I was excited and ready to finish off my two years at a really good university. I was finally able to celebrate moving on.

Then, I received a phone call that changed my life. I answered the phone and heard, "Hello. This is Karen Aston at The University of Texas." I do not even remember the rest of the conversation. I was then faced with another problem. I had already committed to Arkansas, but my dream and my goal was to play in the Big 12, specifically, at Texas. This was the same coach who offered me a scholarship at North Texas the year before.

The University of Texas coach had resigned and Coach Aston took over that position. What a coincidence. Or not. The night before signing, I talked to my parents and they told me that I needed to do what's best for me and have no regrets. I knew that I did not want to go back on my word, no matter how much I knew that Texas was my dream come true.

I knew I needed to deal with this next phone call. "Hey, how did the signing go? Are you excited to be a Razorback?" the coach asked. "Coach, I am so sorry, but I have decided to become a Longhorn. I will be attending The University of Texas." Click. Yes, she hung up in my face. Maybe I could have called her before signing, or maybe I could have done something different. Who knows? All I knew was that it was over. I was going to my dream school. Onto college again. For free. Disclaimer: Coach Aston didn't know I committed to Arkansas when she contacted me. It was a verbal commitment to Arkansas.

Not only was I able to play basketball at the collegiate level, I was able to gain lifetime friends, build relationships with the staff members and fans at my school and receive an education debt-free. FYI, tuition at The University of Texas would have been over $100k for four years.

Having back problems with scoliosis, my ACL injury, causing me to have surgery in one of the most important seasons of my high school career, and dealing with life as a teenager, I still managed to get a free athletic scholarship. More importantly, that free scholarship had opened up opportunities for me to do some amazing things as an entrepreneur. What are you waiting on? Get to work!

IT'S IN
YOUR COURT

➤ Each week, research at least three schools you would like to attend. Research the school's tuition and fees, as well as what scholarships you can receive to help pay for school.

_____

_____

_____

_____

➤ Are you taking your sport seriously enough to receive a scholarship for free education? If not, what is holding you back?

_____

_____

_____

➤ Besides sports, what do you like to do in your spare time? List five things.

_____

_____

_____

_____

➤ If sports were taken out of the picture, what could you see yourself doing?

_____

_____

_____

_____

Notes

_____

_____

_____

_____

_____

_____

_____

_____

_____

_____

_____

_____

Part Two

IN SEASON

WHAT ARE YOU LEARNING
THROUGHOUT THE GAME?

What are you learning from sports? Can tools and strategies learned through sports be applied to everyday life? In this section, we dive into five different things you learn and application strategies to use for your benefit.

There are many ways sports impacted my life. I mean, by playing for over 18 years, you would think so. Right?

Chapter 6

WHERE DID TIME GO? — TIME MANAGEMENT

"Use your time wisely. Time is what we want most, but what we use worst."
- William Penn

G et up. Go to school. Go to all of your classes. Head over to shoot around for game day. Get ready for the game. Play the game. Over by 9:00 pm. Get home and do homework. Eat. Shower. Sleep. Get right back up for school the next day.

Strength and conditioning practice at 5:00 am. Done at 6:30 am. Shower, get dressed, eat - all before 8:00 am class. Finish class at 9:30 am. Next class at 10:00 am. Finish by 11:30 am. Eat lunch by 12:00 pm. Race over to study hall for my 1:00 pm tutor. Get on the bus and head to the gym for 3:00 pm practice. First stop is the weight room. Once done, it's time to go to the gym. Finish practice around 6:00 pm. Go home, shower, do homework and in bed by 9:00 pm, depending on the night. Repeat and do it all over again.

Yep, that was a typical day for me, give or take. Sometimes, study hall was at different times, classes at different times on different days, and longer practices, depending on the coach's mood that day. Playing collegiate sports definitely helped me to understand the importance of managing my time. It quickly helped me to understand that time is something you do not get back, so make the most of it.

Practice, eating at least three times a day, study hall, classes, workouts, sleeping, games, pre-game routines, homework, social time (if any, ha ha), are all things you have to balance while playing college ball. You either adjust or you get lost. It's that simple.

It's 5:00 am and the baby cries. Feed baby. Get baby dressed for daycare. Dress yourself for work. Take baby to daycare. Make it to work on time. Work nine hours. Leave work and pick baby up. Go home and cater to baby. Baby finally falls asleep. Shower yourself. Get in bed to sleep. Baby wakes up crying. Repeat the process.

Wake up. Take kids to school. Go to work. Leave work and pick up kids from school. Kid one has a basketball game and kid two has a soccer game. Arrange for both kids to make their events. Choose which event you will attend. Leave events and go home. Kids take out homework and complete. Get dinner ready for yourself and kids. Eat dinner, wash dishes and clean the kitchen. Get kids ready for school the next day. Everyone showers. Go to sleep. Wake up. Repeat.

Does it all sound familiar to sports? Playing sports prepares you to manage your time in all aspects of life whether job, kids, or relationships. It helps you think about the decisions you are going to make before making them. Will I have enough time to do this if I do that? This is a question I ask myself all the time!

As a high school athlete, I had to manage school work, playing sports, my other siblings playing sports, working out, having a job (yes, I had a job all throughout high school) and having a social life.

Speaking of a job, I was not forced to get a job, nor did I have to get a job. But, when you want to do for yourself and do not like hearing the word no, that's what you do.

I remember it so vividly. Right after practice, I would rush to the locker room and grab my things so I could go home and take a quick shower in time for work. When I would come out of the school, my mom would be right there waiting for me. She always asked me, "How are you going to go to work with your hair still wet?" I always answered saying, "by the time I get to work, it will be dry." Sometimes it was and sometimes it wasn't.

Black shirt, black pants, black belt. My work attire would already be laid out for me once I got home. I worked at Cheddar's Scratch Kitchen as a hostess from my freshman year until my senior year. Disclaimer: I was so good at my job that the manager moved me to take the 'to go' orders where I was making more money and having more fun!

I would go to school, go to practice, leave practice and go work at Cheddar's from 6:00 pm to 10:00 pm, go home, do homework, take a shower, go to sleep and repeat the process. Most times, practice finished around 5:00 pm, so I would knock out some of my homework in between practice and waiting on my mom to pick me up. You know my dad had to say something about me working though. We made a deal that I could keep my job if my grades and performance on the court did not take a backseat.

I made sure that it didn't. But anytime he thought "I played bad" he would say, "That's why you don't need that da** job." My mom would play the good cop and whisper to me, "In one ear and out the other," ha ha. Not that she was telling me not to listen to my dad, but she knew when he was right and also when he was wrong.

My team would win the game, I have a couple points, steals, rebounds and assists and he would spend hours talking about one lay-up I missed. He would say that it was because I was too focused on working at Cheddars. In one ear and out the other, I would think to myself.

College, on the other hand, was a different ball game. Basketball was my job. Somehow, I even managed to coach other select teams while in college and volunteer at multiple events. As mentioned above, in college, there are an ample number of things that you have to manage.

Once season actually started, and we started playing games, the load increased. Workouts at 5:00 am disappeared, but longer practices occurred, game day routines, traveling for games, getting back late and still having to wake up and go to class the next day. Yeah being a college athlete doesn't sound all that easy. Does it? Imagine traveling to Iowa State playing a 7:00 pm game that ended around 10:00 pm. Leaving the gymnasium to catch your flight back to Austin, arriving at 1:00 am, getting home around 1:30 am, taking a shower and getting ready for bed by 2:00 am, having to wake up and be at class at 8:00 am, was the ultimate struggle.

Being involved in athletics teaches you time management, one way or another. No matter what level you are playing at, there is always going to be some type of schedule you have to follow and you are always going to have to balance school with your sport. After all, you are a student-athlete. Time management was something I initially struggled with once graduating from college. The schedule that I once followed was now a schedule that I had to make on my own.

Once I viewed my life as a sport, I was able to shift gears and manage my time better. Although my schedule still consisted of some of the same things it did while I was playing sports, it is now at a much higher level. I am currently getting my master's, running a business in leagues, teams, and camps with a snippet of real estate.

I have to carve out time for school, business, learning, reading, church activities, exercise, eating, sleeping and just a tad bit for shopping! You will realize, as you continue to live life, that the better you are at managing your time, the more successful you will be.

IT'S IN
YOUR COURT

➤ Are you confident in your ability to manage your time well each day?

_____

_____

_____

_____

➤ Do you take time to sit and plan what is most important to you to accomplish each day?

_____

_____

_____

_____

➤ Do you tend to over-plan or under-plan and does that result in you becoming confused or discouraged?

_____

_____

_____

_____

➤ What are some things you can do to help yourself to improve in managing your time?

_____

_____

_____

_____

Notes

_____

_____

_____

_____

_____

_____

_____

_____

_____

_____

Chapter 7

MAKE IT HAPPEN – SACRIFICE

"You have to fight to reach your dream.
You have to sacrifice and work hard for it."
- Lionel Messi

The season starts and I am the starting point guard. I have sacrificed many things for this moment; from being in the gym late at night shooting, to getting to the gym 30 minutes early before practice, to changing my eating habits a bit, to getting more rest to be ready for practices. I was excited to get the year going at my dream school.

That didn't last very long. I was only able to play 16 games that year. I suffered an injury while playing at the University of Oklahoma. It was my knee, again. The same knee as the ACL. I had to have microfracture surgery on my knee this time. I was out for the season, again. Junior year in high school and now junior year in college. Did I spend some time moping around and feeling sorry for myself? You can bet your money I did! Who wouldn't? Here I was playing where I most dreamed of playing. It now seemed like I was dreaming again. The moping stage didn't last for long, but I would be misleading you if I said it didn't happen.

There are a ton of sacrifices you have to make when playing sports. Some you will look back on and be grateful for the choices you made. There may be other choices that you wished you had made differently. In high school, I wasn't able to go to all the football games, nor was I able to hang out with my friends as much as I wanted to. I either had games, practice or work. When I didn't have those things, I was probably studying or doing homework. I am not saying that I never got to hang out, only that my opportunities were rare compared to the rest of my friends. It was a sacrifice I had to make if I wanted to take this basketball thing seriously. Looking back, I do wish my parents were a tad bit lenient on letting me be with my friends and finding that balance in basketball and social life.

I am here to tell you that you can't have it all, but you can have a piece of it. You are going to have to make some sacrifices and miss some things that you may not want to miss at the moment. However, it will be rewarding for you, and at some point, you will be able to enjoy those same things you wish you had done before.

The first question you must ask yourself is, "What do I want?" Is it to be popular? To have all the friends? To go to every event? To play sports? To get a scholarship playing sports? Second, you should ask yourself, "What am I willing to give up to get what I want?" This is not to say that if you want a scholarship, then you have to give up everything. It is simply to say that you have to cut back on some things. You have to commit yourself to doing that.

There will come times when you have to choose. Go to the football game on Friday night or go to basketball practice on Friday night. The good thing is that all things don't last forever. You may not be able to do something at the moment, but you may be able to do it months from now or next year. Only you can choose. Choose wisely.

Let me rewind here for a bit. Do you even know what sacrifice means? Have you ever wanted to do or have something that conflicted with something else? For example, you have a game Saturday morning, but you want to play Fortnite all Friday night. In doing so, you may be tired and not have the energy for the game because you were up all night.

You now have a tough decision to make. Do you stay up all night playing Fortnite or prepare for the game by getting a good night sleep? Many of you reading this would probably choose Fortnite. However, that wouldn't be the best decision. Indeed, a sacrifice would have to be made. But on the bright side, Fortnite will still be there once you return from playing your game. However, there is no way to undo a poor performance after the game has been played.

One definition of the word "sacrifice" is "the act of giving up something that you want to keep or have, especially in order to get or do something else or to help someone."

Going back to our example above, you would probably have to give up the video game for this one night so that you are prepared for your game the next day. It could be as simple as choosing not to play the game until 2:00 am and instead stop playing at 9:00 pm in order to be well rested for tomorrow's game.

It is important that we not only learn to make sacrifices that will benefit ourselves, but also those that will benefit others.

In a team environment, athletes must sacrifice what they want to strenghten others, as well as the team. No one player can have their way and make decisions based on their own wants. Have you ever played with someone who hogged the ball all the time? Or pushed you out of the way to get in front? Or someone who always insisted in being the one who was in the bright lights? As someone who is a part of a team, whether in sports or in any group effort, selfishness never wins.

If you are reading this book, then you have most likely been a part of a team before. Each of us possess strengths and weaknesses. It is important to understand what they are in order to effectively contribute to the team. For instance, if you are not a great shooter, but your teammate who is wide open is, you may have to pass up an open shot to get them the better shot. That is what making sacrifices and being a team player is all about.

Life is all about choices; you get to decide what you're willing to give up to gain the things that you cherish most. If you want more playing time, what sacrifices are you willing to make to achieve it? Are you willing to go to the gym not only when you want to, but also when you don't want to? Have a consistent workout schedule? Being able to make sacrifices is a quality that promotes growth for the greater good.

IT'S IN
YOUR COURT

➤ What are some sacrifices you have had to make to get where you are now?

_____

_____

_____

_____

➤ What sacrifices do you think you will still need to make in order to get what you want? (Making the team next year, making varsity, starting on varsity, getting a scholarship, etc.)

_____

_____

_____

➤ Write down at least three things you are willing to sacrifice to help yourself to reach your goals.

_____

_____

_____

_____

➤ Are you willing to sacrifice for others? Why or why not?

_____

_____

_____

_____

Notes

Chapter 8

LET'S PLAY THE TALKING GAME – COMMUNICATION

*"The single biggest problem in communication is
the illusion that it has taken place."*
- George Bernard Shaw

Out of all the traits we talk about, communication may just be my favorite. Communication is key in every aspect of your life and sports allow you to check that off your toolbox. The more you play sports and move up levels, the more you will see how big communication really is. How do you know if someone is open for the ball? They yell, "Ball"! How does someone know if you need help because your defender went passed you? You yell, "Help"!

Coach: *High knees*

Players: *High knees (claps twice)*

Coach: *Butt kicks*

Players: *But kicks (claps twice)*

Coach: *Frankenstein*

Players: *Frankenstein (claps twice)*

Coach: *Lay-ups*

Player: *Lay-ups! Sprints to half-court like our life depends on it.*

Ball rolls on the ground.

Players: *Loose Loose * runs to pick up the ball*

Coach: *Z-drill*

Players: *Z-drill * ball, ball, ball, ball saying constantly until our mouth is dry and can't say anymore*

Every drill that our coach called out, we repeated. Not only that, we always encouraged each other and talked throughout the entire practice. "Good job ladies", "keep working", "you got this", and "good shot" are just some of the many things we said to each other constantly during practice. Communicating in practice led to communicating in the game.

This leads to communicating in life. Communication is a trait that not everyone picks up. Not everyone is put in a position where they have to learn how to communicate with others. But athletes are. Athletes are forced to communicate with each other at all times. You have to be able to communicate at school, at your job, in your relationships, with your kids and the list goes on. What better way to pick up this skill than through sports?

Sometimes you have to learn this lesson the hard way – like many tough lessons sports teach us.

During my JUCO days at South Plains, we were in conference play and we are up against Howard College. They had already beat us once that season at the buzzer, and it was all because we did not communicate. To make a long story short, Howard had the ball to take the last shot. They ran their best shooter off a screen and we didn't call the screen nor switch as our coach told us to. Swish. Nothing but net. She was wide open.

Time for round two. This was probably the best game we played all season, and it started with one thing. Communication.

On the defensive end, all five players on the court were talking to each other.

"I got your help, Ashley."

"Baseline runner, baseliner runner. She's coming high."

Those are just some of the things that were said throughout the game. Not to mention the entire bench calling screens, yelling shooter and getting excited. We came out on top that night. It is amazing how communicating with each other makes the game that much easier.

It is music to a coach's ears to hear the team communicating with each other. Effective communication limits mistakes on the court and leads to more opportunities to succeed.

I can guarantee that every player has had this short, simple conversation with their coach before:

Player: *Coach, I was open.*

Coach: *Did you call for the ball?*

Player: *No.*

Coach: *Then you were not open.*

As a coach, I see firsthand how athletes seem to love playing sports without communicating. Calling for the ball when open could not only lead to two points to help advance your team's score, but also leads to you being able to score more points. Let's be honest, who doesn't love to score?

Fear keeps us quiet. So don't be afraid to let your voice be heard. It's very likely the exact thing your team needs.

Communication is not only about how you communicate with someone, but also about how you receive it. It was important for us to communicate with each other throughout the game but just as important to receive it the way it was delivered. You have to be able to give and receive. Some only know how to communicate what they want, but don't know or understand how to receive communication given to them. It almost goes hand in hand with feedback. Feedback is a form of communication, rather for good or bad. How do you get that message across? How do you receive that message? You know that teammate that wants to always tell you what to do but doesn't want to listen to anything you tell them to do? Yeah, I had plenty of those. They were so good about communicating with you, good or bad, but did not want to receive it back.

Truthfully, I was never that great at receiving information. My high school coach would always say, "Just one day, Ashley, just one day," as in just one day you will listen to me. My problem was I believed she was against me and did not like me. Anything she communicated to me was taken in a negative way and her tone came across as if she was trying to embarrass me in front of the team.

It didn't take long for me to realize the tone in her voice was actually the passion she had for me to succeed. The constructive criticism was only for me to do better and not make the same mistakes repeatedly. She would often say to me, "If I ever stop correcting you, then you should be worried."

Communication is not just about what you say, but also how you say it. When she would tell me things in a loud voice or use her hands to communicate her thoughts, I would feel horrible about myself. What I didn't understand at the time was the passion and belief she had in me to fix it and get it right.

Through my experiences, I learned communication can be verbal or nonverbal, such as using your hands, feet, etc., to get your message across. Naturally, if my coaches stomped their feet while talking, I would get uptight and think they are upset. If my teammate yelled at me during practice, you could forget about me talking to her for a few days. This was due to the fact that I did not understand every message being communicated will not always be conveyed in a soft or friendly manner. Sometimes, especially during the heat of the moment, a message may come off as harsh or rude. In reality, we must learn how to listen to what is being delivered as opposed to how it is being delivered.

Good communication skills are key to success in life, work and relationships. Without effective communication, a message can turn into a misunderstanding, frustration or even disaster by being misinterpreted or poorly delivered. I have to constantly communicate with parents, players and my coaches to keep things running as smoothly as possible.

Know what you want to say and why. Understand the purpose and intent of your message. Know to whom you are communicating and why. Think about sports for an example. When I played, I had some teammates who could take constructive criticism well and others I had to make sure I was careful with how I said things because they might get offended. Consider any barriers you may encounter such as cultural differences or situational circumstances (gender, age, or economic biases). Ask yourself what outcome you want to achieve and the impression you want to leave.

Most of us do more talking than listening. What is it that makes us more concerned about what we are going to say than what the other person is saying to us? Take the time to really listen to what people are saying, by their words, tone and body language. If they know you are really listening to them, they will be more open and trust you with their real thoughts and feelings. Ask questions about what they are saying to encourage them to open up more. The more you really listen, the more they will open up, the more you really listen, the more they will open up... and the cycle goes on.

When you take the time to acquire and hone good communication skills, you open yourself up to better relationships, more career opportunities and increased self-confidence. Moreover, you reach higher levels of mutual understanding and cooperation while successfully attaining your goals. All new skills take time to refine; however, with effort and practice you can develop good, even exceptional, communication skills.

IT'S IN
YOUR COURT

➤ Think about the different ways you communicate with yourself. Do you talk to yourself? Do you say nice things to yourself? Do you encourage yourself with words? Do you beat yourself up?

_____

_____

_____

_____

➤ Think about the different ways you communicate with others. How does this compare to how you communicate with yourself?

_____

_____

_____

➤ What are some of the different ways you communicate with your teammates while playing your sport? For example, verbal, hands, facial expressions.

_____

_____

_____

_____

➤ In all the various ways people communicate with each other, do you feel comfortable in your ability to connect with others and to get your message across? Why?

_____

_____

_____

_____

Notes

Chapter 9

IT TAKES MORE THAN YOU – TEAMWORK

"Teamwork divides the task and multiplies the success."
- Author Unknown

Together Everyone Achieves More. TEAM. No matter the sport you are a part of, you are a team. That is probably one of the most exciting things about playing sports. You get to be a part of something much bigger than yourself. This team thing allows you to gain new sisters and brothers each year. Your team becomes those you spend the majority of your time with. They become family.

For me, some of my teammates will be the same ones in my wedding and planning my baby shower. Whenever that time comes. Being on a team not only allows you to be a part of something bigger than you, but it also surrounds you with other like-minded individuals.

In basketball, you have five positions on the court. The point guard, shooting guard, small forward, power forward and center. You wouldn't expect the center to play the point guard spot and the point guard to play the center spot. Each person has a specific role on the team. It doesn't mean that players can't play different positions, but it does mean they can't play different positions at the same time. To win games, you have to work as a team. All five people on the court have to work collectively in order to work towards winning games.

That brings up another important point about being on a team. Everyone is working towards one common goal. That could be to make it to the playoffs. It could be to win one game, to win a tournament, to win a state championship or to win a national championship. Either way, everyone is working towards accomplishing something as a team.

Every year before season, we would take a walk to the room. The room was a room we went to and talked about the upcoming season and our goals. Every year, I had that bubbly feeling in my stomach walking into the room. As we would walk in there, there would be big binders on our chairs waiting on us to open. Once we sat down, it was time to focus on one thing and one thing only. "Welcome! It's here. Season is finally here," Coach Aston would say. "Open up your notebooks and let's get started," she continued.

We would go over our goals. We would break up our goals into smaller pieces. We had team, conference, season and team academic goals. That would set the tone on how we wanted the season to go. What was important was that we set realistic goals. If the year before we had a losing season, we didn't say we wanted to win a national championship. Of course, everyone wants to do that, but we made sure we set ourselves up for success by first setting attainable goals. Coach would ask us and we would come up with our goals as a whole. That was the fun part!

When you are done with sports and have to get a job, nine times out of ten, you will be a part of a team or you will have to work in a team setting. Being a part of a team for so many years will have you prepared and ready to tackle any assignments coming your way. You will be amazed at how many people do not know how to work as team, simply because they have never had to. Being a part of a team takes some of the stress and pressure off you to get everything done yourself. You can divide assignments throughout your team. Just as in sports.

Basketball is made up of a whole team. Players, coaches, strength coaches, etc. Our head coach at The University of Texas was not in the weight room showing us how to do exercises. That was the strength coach's job. She was simply there to support and clap for us. Nothing more, nothing less. Our trainer wasn't on the sidelines trying to coach us and tell us plays to run. She was there in case of an injury or if someone needed some type of medical assistance. That is the benefit of having a team and being a part of one helps you understand that concept much quicker.

With everything comes challenges, right?

Learning to be a team player can be a challenge and something that has to be learned. Certainly, in sports you have to learn that it is not all about you. If you are not scoring all the points that night, but your teammate is, you should be excited for them.

If one person messes up in a drill, and there are consequences for it, most times the entire team will do those consequences, and not just the one who messed up. It can be challenging. Most times, you want to be the one in the spotlight, or you don't want to have consequences for someone else's mistakes. Learning to be a team player teaches you important skills and holds you accountable for your actions. You then start to think about not being the one to mess up and make everyone run or not being the one that has bad grades and bring the team GPA down.

These same challenges show up in many areas of life. They will come in the classroom when having to do team projects, or in the work force when dealing with other coworkers. Challenges will show up when having to deal with anything in a team setting. You will find that others either do not know how to work on a team or simply don't want to because they are not accustomed to the team setting. You will find that most people are very selfish or when granted the opportunity to work with others feel they can place all the work on one person and reap the benefits. This can be a challenge for athletes who have always worked on a team and understand how to work as a team to accomplish one common goal. We tend to become frustrated when others are not able to work as a team and it can be a challenge.

IT'S IN
YOUR COURT

➤ Do you find it challenging or difficult for you to work on a team, whether that is in your sport or on a group project? If so, why?

_____

_____

_____

_____

➤ What are some character traits that are necessary to be successful working with others?

_____

_____

_____

➤ What are the strengths you bring that contribute to the success of your team?

_____

_____

_____

_____

➤ How has being a part of a team helped you throughout your life?

_____

_____

_____

_____

Notes

Chapter 10

PREPARE TO WIN OR PREPARE TO LOSE

"By failing to prepare, you are preparing to fail."
- **Benjamin Franklin**

Junior year at The University of Texas was by far the hardest year of my life. I won't get into all of that now; that can be a whole book in itself! You think you have it all figured out until something new or different arises. For me, it was transitioning from junior college to Division I. I was still playing basketball and going to school. I still had a schedule to follow. Yet, everything seemed much different and so much faster than at South Plains. The key was preparation.

At South Plains, I was able to do as I pleased for the most part. Wake up, go to a few classes, go eat, head to practice and go home. When we had games, we would watch film on them, but that was it. We would only watch.

At Texas, our film sessions were however long the coach wanted for us to be in there. We had a scout on the team that had every player on there, what the team likes to do and doesn't like to do. The players' strengths, weaknesses, and so forth. We knew all about the team before ever seeing the team. She was preparing us for our opponents. When we had practice, we had to go to the training room first to heat our bodies up or get taped. Preparing for practice. After practice, we had to take an ice bath. Boy, I did not like those, but it was good for the body.

Senior year was here and I was trying to get back in the swing of things. My knee just would not let me be great. It started giving me problems during season and I was in some serious pain. It was my last year, so I kept pushing and fighting through the pain. It wasn't until the Texas Tech game that I couldn't take anymore. I finally went to the doctor and was told that if I did not want to have a knee replacement by the age of 30, I would have to hang it up. That was one of the hardest decisions that I ever had to make. Another year. Season over.

I had been through knee problems countless times. All I wanted to do was to finish my basketball career playing the game that bought me a free education. It was either that or my knee. My knee won. As much as I wanted to play, I couldn't imagine having a knee replacement at such a young age or walking around with a cane. As hard as this was, it was time to put basketball to rest. After all, I used it to get what I wanted and that was a free education. I knew my playing days would be over once I graduated from college. What I didn't know was that my career ending injury was preparing me for the next phase in my life.

It was preparing me to be a coach. I had more free time to coach youth teams, go to the coach's office and ask countless questions, see the behind-the-scenes of coaching, etc. During the games, I was like the coach of the coach. I would help my teammates and show them things I saw from the bench that they couldn't see because they were in the game. My senior year was molding me for my profession.

Shortly after graduating, I got my first real job as a middle school teacher and coach. One year later, I was the head varsity coach at Cedar Creek High School. A few years later, I was successfully running my own business that still involved coaching, but more directed to the youth. Coaching has always been a part of me and that senior year prepared me for those moments.

What do you need to do in order to ace the test you have coming up this week? Are you going to start looking at the material the night before? No, you are going to prepare for it. You study the night before and every night before that. That is the way you set yourself up for success in passing the test.

How are you going to win your upcoming game? Make sure you are prepared. You have a big interview coming up. You need to make sure you are prepared to land the job. Anything you do requires preparation! That is one of the main tools you will have in your tool belt from being involved in sports. One of my coaches used to always say, "Stay ready, so you don't have to get ready," and that is something I live by today.

If you are always ready for what is to come, you don't have to spend so much time trying to get ready for it. Let me break it down a little further for you. If you are running a 5k in two months, are you just going to wait until that day comes and go run it? Well, you can, but you probably wouldn't get the outcome you want. However, if you start training and preparing your mind and your body for the race, you will put yourself in a position to do well.

IT'S IN
YOUR COURT

➤ Is preparation important to you? Why?

_____

_____

_____

_____

➤ How do you prepare for upcoming tests and exams or presentations and meetings?

_____

_____

_____

_____

➤ How do you prepare for upcoming games?

_____

_____

_____

_____

➤ How can preparation help you throughout your life?

_____

_____

_____

_____

Notes

Part Three

POST/OFF SEASON

Beware: You are about to enter the space of all interviewees.

Following are perspectives from athletes who have been there and done that – hear from those who have successfully changed lanes and from coaches who help us all transition from one phase to the next.

Part Three

POST /OFF SEASON

Chapter 11

INTERVIEWS WITH ATHLETES

RICKY BROWN

AMBER QUIST

A. J. ABRAMS

CAT OSTERMAN

MARK HENRY

RICKY BROWN

STATS

SPORTS CAREER:

➤ The University of Texas Football Team, 1996 - 1999 (Participated in 1997 Fiesta Bowl, 1999 & 2000 Cotton Bowls)

➤ Started 30 of last 32 Games

➤ Three Straight 1000 Yard Rushes

➤ 1999 Team Co-Captain

➤ NFL Professional Football Player - Cincinnati Bengals - Two Seasons

PROFESSIONAL CAREER:

➤ SMU – Finance

➤ JP Morgan, Vice President for Client Investments, New York, NY

➤ Assistant Athletics Director for T-Association; Player Development & Fundraising

INTERVIEW

What was your first experience for life after sports?

My first experience was really dealing with, "Who will I be after this is gone?" The easiest way I can describe it is it feels completely uncertain. I mean, for all of your life that you can remember, you've had that sport as a cornerstone of your identity, your success, your ability. You now have to quickly figure out, "What am I going to do?" "What am I going to be good at?" My first job was working in the front office of semi-pro teams, as I was trying to figure out what my skill set was.

I would say, "Can I work in the front office in sales? Can I help with tickets and those kinds of things?" That was while I was still playing, but I could see that the end was coming. I wanted to transition to something else, so I started working in those front offices to do that. But my real shock and awe was going back to business school and being in a classroom after having played for roughly four or five seasons, and going right back into the classroom at SMU. It was like, okay, football's definitely no longer a part of my life right now.

What are some examples of how you may have failed before gaining the momentum you have?

Well, I talked about working in the front office and sales. It positioned me to focus on the sales route. One of the first jobs that I took was in copier sales. I can remember, I played for Coach Brown here at Texas, and I thought that I just needed to leverage my contacts to secure this job. It was a company called Lanier Worldwide. If you don't know anything about copier sales, it's the hardest of the hard, because copiers last for forever. It's a completely commoditized business, which means, from provider to provider, there isn't a lot of differentiation. And people are usually saving; they're stepping over dollars to save pennies, when it comes to copier machines. And it's a door-to-door sales type role.

So, I got a lot of no's; a lot of rejection. I had to learn very quickly to get over feeling like I was something special. I just had to plow through the rejections and understand that it was going to be the key to me getting to my numbers or having any success at all. That job lasted a year and a half.

I tried to go back and play again. It was like, "Oh my God, this is incredibly tough. Is this really what I want to do?" I played for another season in semi-professional football, and I said, "You know what, I'm not going back to that life. I want to go and make sure I finish my degree, because I'm done with football." That was what it took for me to say, "I'm completely done." I needed to invest in what my next steps were going to be.

What do you think three benefits of playing sports are?

I would say, dealing with high-pressure situations is a huge benefit of participating in sports, particularly in collegiate sports. You're going to have to make decisions in high-pressure situations, like when the game is on the line. And that's hard to replicate in real life, high-pressure situations. But you get it in sports. And so, that's a huge advantage, because your thought process can be significantly altered when the adrenaline level goes up. So, I think just having some experience in those high-pressure situations helped me make good decisions, stay calm and relaxed.

When I was in New York on Wall Street, and companies were losing value, and shareholders were asking me what to do with their assets, to have been in and competed in high-pressured situations, those scenarios paled in comparison. So that's one advantage.

Another is developing and honing a competitive mindset where you understand what it's like to have teammates and you are all striving to be the best you can possibly be. So, you know how to work with others, that you might be competing against in some sense, but you are also helping them to get better, helping yourself to get better, so that overall, the team is better. And I think that the competitive mindset, while being part of a team, is also something that's very hard to replicate. It's hard to find, frankly, in the real world, once you leave competitive sports.

The third benefit is the level of practice and repetition, deliberate practice. In order to become really great at anything, you have to immerse yourself in it. You have to perform deliberate practice, day in and day out. And I took that from my sports background. If you're going to become great, if you're going to become a master at something, or really skilled, you've got to devote that kind of time and attention to it and focus. I think those are really important aspects of sports that are built into that environment and culture that are really beneficial.

What is one principle that you have learned throughout sports that has helped prepare you for your life today?

I would say it's how to deal with adversity. Sports put me through serious injuries. It's like Mike Tyson's quote, which I love, "Everyone has a plan until you get hit in the face." And that's what sports does.

It hits you in the face and it forces you to deal with adversity in a way that's really tangible and very transparent.

In other words, oftentimes, you're a part of a team, or you're competing in a public type environment, and you have to deal with being benched. Or you have to deal with not being the starter. Or you might have to deal with playing out of the position you thought you wanted to play in.

I think the ways you deal with those things are the formulation of your character. Sports really taught me how to deal with extreme adversity, overcoming an injury, and dealing with having to work your way back to where you want to be.

If you could go back and talk to yourself as a college athlete, what would you say to yourself that could help prepare you for life today?

When you are a collegiate athlete, it feels like that is everything. And if I could over time impart something, some idea, it would be that this is not everything. It's not the end all be all. It is where you are right now in your life. But you're on a long journey; you're on a long marathon. And this moment might feel like everything, it might feel like it is the center of the universe so to speak, but there is a lot more to life, and there's a lot more to your life that will be important.

What would you say to yourself as a high school athlete?

I would tell myself to meet people, be open about who you are, be engaging and enjoy the experience. I would say that also at the college level. Enjoy the experience, enjoy the environment and try to connect with as many people as you possibly can.

What do you believe are three key traits that athletes pick up from sports?

I'd say coach-ability. Athletes in particular, pick up coach-ability or the ability to deal with critical feedback. I think that's something that can be very difficult for folks who haven't been in sports, for somebody to come at you and say, "You're doing this all wrong." Well guess what, athletes hear that almost every day. So, you develop a thick skin, and an ability to handle criticism. This is critical to getting better, right? That's how you get better, by taking in that feedback.

I think there's another trait you find in athletes. They understand what it means to be fully committed to something. In order to be good and to be competitive at the college level, especially at a top university, they understand how committed they have to be to that craft. I think commitment is something that can be hard to teach. What is your level of commitment? I would say that's another trait that you find in athletes, particularly collegiate athletes. They understand what it means to have a high level of commitment. And I guess it could go hand-in-hand with commitment, but discipline. The day in and day out of applying discipline to what you want to accomplish.

How does playing sports translate to your respective career?

I've had a couple of careers since sports. I would say that my career in finance is very similar. You see a lot of former athletes that migrate to the finance space. It's because of the competitive nature of finance. It is also because finance is very numbers driven. If you think about sports, how much of sports is statistics and numbers and production? It's very similar when you look at businesses. Businesses are about revenue, how much did that company make and in valuing companies.

And then there's the sales aspect, which I think of as being leadership. When you're in a sales environment, what you're really trying to accomplish is leadership, whether it's with clients or with your fellow colleagues. Sales is a form of leadership. It's saying, "Come walk down this path with me." I really felt like even though I was in finance, some of what I was doing was leadership and sales.

In the role that I'm in now, I deal a lot with athletes that are in transition. That is in fact a lot of my focus. It's the experience of going from being a professional athlete and a college athlete and dealing with the identity crisis of, "Okay, my sport is not going to help me, necessarily. My sport is not going to be there for me to make money forever."

And then, understanding how I could redevelop or transition and use transferable skills that I developed in sports to build a new identity for myself and a new career path.

What I try to do in my current role is help impart those same ideas and concepts to the student athletes that are dealing with those same issues.

If you have an athlete come to you for advice, what is your one piece of advice that would help them think beyond being just an athlete?

It depends on the individual I think. My approach would be to try and understand what they love about athletics. Sometimes it's the competitive nature. At other times, it's their ability to work with the team. I think you can find out a lot about who a person is by what drives them and what drives them to certain things. Once I have an understanding of what that person loves about sports, I would say to look at other areas where you see those same things in you, and understand that sports is not the only place where that exists. It just might be the one that's driving your life right now.

I would also encourage them to take an interest in current events. Understand what's happening in the world outside of the world of sports. Know that you might not always be in just the sports world. You may be in a completely different industry in a few years, particularly if you're a collegiate athlete. We know what the numbers are there. So, think about other interests that you have, and particularly when you're on campus. That's a perfect place to explore other interests.

What are the first three steps that you would advise an athlete on to prepare them to change lanes and to start thinking about life after sports?

Oh, my gosh. I think this is true, no matter what you do, to sustain yourself, I would say to develop some hobbies, things that you enjoy outside of your sport that are really fun for you. Whether that's collecting things, whether that's some form of art or expression. A number of guys that I've played with, music was a part of them and they took music classes. And they had taken up an instrument. I'd even them tell that I don't know what I would have done without music during those times, because it was just a way for me to let loose and deal with the pressure. I would say developing a hobby is one really good thing that can help you transition and help you connect with your identity outside of sports.

I would also say to try to expand your network. As you come across people with similar interests, be proactive about staying in contact with them and developing relationships. That's a really important one. And I think that goes for all levels. But it's not as easy to meet people once you leave campus as it was when you were on campus. You almost take for granted how many people you will come in contact with on a daily basis when you're in college. And then, once you leave, that number dramatically drops. So, it's just something you want to be mindful of.

One of the things that I talk about in my book is FTA. I call it a disease that most athletes get once they finish playing. It's called "First Thing Available". People just jump into the first thing available because they don't know what to do. Did you experience FTA? If so, what action steps did you take to get out of it? If not, what did you do to avoid it?

I think it goes back to the mentors that you have in your life. I don't know that I avoided it completely. In hindsight, I feel like I reached the point of understanding what some of my skills were by talking to mentors, asking for their advice, trying to understand what they saw. You're going to get different answers that way. Then what you have to do is to make a decision, you have to choose based on what you feel. And, it's hard if you're starting again.

When you're starting out fresh with building a new skill set, it's hard to know what is going to work or exactly which direction you should take. I've found that people who know you well, but have an outside-in view, can be very valuable at helping you piece together what your skill sets are. And you're doing this at an age where you're still really young in most cases. I think the best thing you can do is try to get advice from as many people as you can that you trust and that know you. I think that'll help you navigate. And, I mean as many as you can. That is what helps you avoid the first person who says to you, "Oh my gosh, you should go into fashion." Or, "You should start a t-shirt company." Ask more than just one or two people that you trust. That goes back to the idea of building out your network and meeting a lot of folks. Over time, you're going to want to ask some of those folks, your mentors and your close friends for advice.

I also want to say that I think it's important to have mentors and people that you connect with that are not at your same level. You just need people who have perspective. You're going to have some good friends that are at your level, that are really smart, that are killing it. And yes, it's going to be helpful for you to talk to them. But I also think talking with someone who's older, who's walked in your shoes, your footsteps, is going to be really valuable for you to get perspective on life afterwards, and what you can do to position yourself.

As a financial professional, I worked a lot with people who were reaching retirement, approaching retirement, and I found their perspectives and their advice to be so valuable in terms of how you look back on your life versus how you look forward. And the person that you want to try to serve and position well is you; five years from now, and ten years from now. What would you, ten years from now, be telling you now about your life and the things that are important to you? You need that perspective. That is often hard to get from people who are at your same age and stage in life.

What does "using sports as a vehicle" mean to you?

It means taking the benefits of sports and maximizing them for the time when sports is no longer going to carry you. That metaphor of a vehicle is a metaphor for carrying you. There's a period of time when sports will be there and carry you. However, in terms of competition, we all know that there's a very short life there. You're going to reach your peak performance in your 20s, maybe 30s, if you're really fortunate. You have that vehicle for that period of time. What you want to do is make sure that you glean every advantage that you can from sports. Whether that's meeting people, whether that's honing your character and your skillset, and understanding what it is about you that will help you lay the foundation for your next chapter of life.

That is what it means for me to use sports as a vehicle. It helped me get to college. I don't know that I would have ever been able to attend a university like UT. And then once you're here, what do you do with that? That to me is using sports as a vehicle. I think you can also use it as a platform. And a lot of people have made incredible social impact by taking the platform that sports provides. I mean, we talk about Colin Kaepernick, but we can go all the way back to Muhammad Ali, right? And you see the power of sports as a platform as well.

AMBER QUIST

STATS

SPORTS CAREER:

➤ The University of Texas Women's Varsity Soccer Team; Captain 2000 - 2001

➤ Big 12 Conference All-Academic Team; 1999 - 2001

PERSONAL/PROFESSIONAL CAREER:

➤ Recognized as Marketing Leader for Growth Companies

➤ Strategic Marketing Leader; Participated in taking Bazaarvoice Public; 2012

➤ Recruited to Lead Marketing for Mass Relevance; Assisted in Growth to 150 People Serving 300 Clients Globally Before Being Acquired in 2014

➤ Recruited to Lead Marketing as CMO of Silvercar; Successfully Building a Team and Leading Through an Acquisition by Audi in 2017

➤ Frequent Speaker on Marketing, Mobility and Female Leadership

➤ Board Member for Generation SERVE

➤ Working Mother of Two Girls (Ages 6 and 4)

INTERVIEW

What was your first experience for life after sports?

I played soccer at The University of Texas from 1998 to 2002. I've always said that nobody quite prepares you for that transition from being a college student-athlete to being out in the world. After college, I was still all consumed with my sport. And frankly, it has a way of becoming your identity; who you think you are. Suddenly, I am not only pursuing something that I want to do, but also, I realize that being an athlete is not necessarily a part of my identity any more. For me, that was a little bit bigger transition than just getting out of college. I was able to transition out of that and then into a job that I enjoyed. However, it was not necessarily the path that I wanted to be on because I hadn't spent much time thinking about that.

What was the job you took that was not the path that you wanted to be on? And why did you get into it?

I wanted to stay in Austin. Since my undergraduate was in business, with a focus in marketing, I took a sales job with a printing company. I knew that I didn't really want to be in sales. But it had provided me with a wider perspective when I went into marketing. I can say I carried a bag and know that side of the business. So, taking this job was a little bit more opportunistic at the time.

What are some examples of how you failed before gaining the momentum you have?

I would consider my first year out of college a failure, because I wasn't prepared to pursue something I really wanted to do. I took something because it came to me. I found myself in a place where I was unhappy, all because I had not prepared. I was letting life happen to me instead of going after life.

Today, I don't look at failure the same way. We learn from our mistakes and as long as we don't let them keep us down, we keep the momentum going. You have to work through the hard times to persevere and get to the other side.

What do you think three benefits of playing sports are?

The first benefit is the ability to be a part of a team. Teamwork is essential for any successful effort. The ability to work with others to reach a goal, where everybody works hard, contributes, pushes each other to be stronger, and holds each other accountable, is invaluable both on the field and in the work world. Learning to lead and influence others is an extension of being a good team player.

The second benefit is having the determination to succeed and the willingness to work hard in order to be good at what you do. This is what I think set me apart, at work and sports, is pure determination and hard work. And those are things that are invaluable. I was always the first person on the field and the last one off. And I think that's the same that has helped me in my career. That has certainly been something that I have found to be a key ingredient for success, is just the willingness to put in the hard work.

Last, is just enjoying pure competition. You don't get to be a collegiate athlete if you aren't competitive. And I think that no matter what it is I've done in my professional career, certainly a lot of it has been driven by just the willingness or desire to win and to be at the top. Whether that's personally, or as a company, I think that competitive nature permeates through what I've done in the companies that I've been a part of.

What is one principle that you have learned throughout sports that has helped prepare you for your life today?

I would say that one principle, or rather two principles put together, are grit and grace. Grit is my determination, that no matter what it takes, I have a "get it done" attitude. That determination has to be surrounded with a certain amount of grace. Grace shows up by having a level of empathy and understanding for other people, being people focused and people centered. Teamwork and learning to work with others is critical for life.

If you could go back and talk to yourself as a college athlete, what would you say to yourself that could help prepare you for life today?

As a college athlete, I would tell myself to be deliberate about my future. I think it's very easy, not just as a college athlete, but just as a college student, to live in the moment. I've spent some time speaking on college campuses in different marketing classes. I find it surprising how few people reach out afterward, even though I put it out there that I am available. It's interesting how few people are thinking, "Hey, here's somebody that's speaking in my class that can be a resource for me as I look for jobs." Such a small percentage of student athletes go on to pursue sports outside of the moment in college. But it's what is all consuming. I, too, didn't spend enough time really thinking about the bigger picture.

What would you say to yourself as a high school athlete?

Probably to continue to invest in academics, as well as sports. I would tell myself to make sure that I spend as much time feeding my brain as I spend feeding my physical abilities for sports.

What do you believe are three key traits that athletes pick up from sports?

I think they pick up a mental toughness; that ability to push through barriers. Athletes also learn how to make the tough choices. It takes making tough choices to not compromise when temptation comes to pull you in directions that are opposite of where you want to go. There are lots of parties, fun and social events that you miss out on.

The benefit of being willing to make sacrifices now for something better later is incredibly important when you get into things that come later in life. Whether that is in relationships, marriage, or decisions when you have to decide to be a working mom.

Having a high level of discipline is probably the third one. When I think about discipline for me today, not only does it mean being dedicated to my work, but also, having the discipline to create boundaries and find a level of sanity and balance in the world that allows me to be a successful mom, a successful wife, and a successful Chief Marketing Officer.

What are the first three steps that you would advise an athlete on to prepare them to change lanes and to start thinking about life after sports?

I don't know if these are in order, but the advice that I would probably give to them is to be bold. I was once told by someone, right out of college, that you don't get what you don't ask for. And I think that has an interesting lens on it, too. When you're talking about females, there's a lot of discussion in the working world today about gender equality. Men typically negotiate on what they think they can achieve and women negotiate based on what they already have achieved. And so, I would say to female athletes, specifically, to be bold. And don't apologize. And to ask for things that you may not feel like you've achieved yet. But to boldly go after what you hope to achieve.

I would say your network is incredibly important. The same person that told me that you don't get what you don't ask for also told me that it doesn't matter who you know. It matters who knows you. And so, I spent a lot of time, especially in this part of the year, re-engaging my network of people. I have not gotten a single job without having known someone. And I hire that way, too. I think the best employees that I hire come from recommendations.

I think that the more people that you can get out and talk to before you leave college, the more equipped and prepared and knowledgeable and connected you are. And the more opportunities that you'll find come your way. So, I would say focus on just talking to people. People love to talk about themselves. So, make it a goal in your senior year to reach out to five people, maybe it's five different fields that you're interested in getting into. Or maybe it's five people in a specific field that you have narrowed in on.

Do the work so that when you graduate you have people that can already be advocates for you. Taking that a step further would be to find a mentor. Find somebody and ask them to be a mentor to you. And be deliberate and aggressive about seeking advice from them. In the same way of building your network is having a mentor, someone who is older than you and is committed to help you in that way. It will be a tremendous benefit to you throughout that transition.

In your profession, can you tell the difference in people who have played sports before and the ones who didn't? If so, what is that difference?

When I am looking to hire someone, seeing somebody that has played sports is a plus, because of all of the reasons that we just talked about. There's a certain level of understanding of dedication, of mental toughness, of perseverance, of competitiveness. And those are all things that I certainly look for when hiring and building teams. However, there are a lot of smart people who haven't played sports, and they are just as important to organizations. So, I don't want to discount that. But certainly, they are great attributes to pull from, which translate directly from the field to a working environment.

One of the things that I talk about in my book is FTA. I call it a disease that most athletes get once they finish playing. It's called "First Thing Available". People just jump into the first thing available because they don't know what to do. Did you experience FTA? If so, what action steps did you take to get out of it? If not, what did you do to avoid it?

First thing available. I like that. I certainly had that approach or, at least, it happened to me. I'll tell you my personal experience. Then I can tell you why I don't know if I would have taken the path again. I went back to school. To be honest, I hit repeat, and part of that was out of fear. Part of it was out of curiosity and exploration.

I didn't feel like I had fully exercised that while I was in school. And part of it was that I was running from an unhappy situation. And so, I went back to school and spent a lot of money to get my master's degree. I certainly valued that time. I would say, if I were advising somebody now, unless you're going to Harvard, or Kellogg, or something, don't spend the money on an MBA. Staying in Austin, and working at start-ups in the tech world, I would have gained as much knowledge, experience, and capabilities just by switching jobs. It wasn't necessary to go back to school.

For people that are looking to get out of their FTA, and school is an option, I recommend they take some time to work so that they have funds to apply to their education rather than take on debt. I wish I had taken a little bit more time, and thought about that a little bit more.

Looking to get out of your FTA? Just go interview people. Go talk to people. Go build and strengthen your network. People like to help other people, especially in a town like Austin, Texas. You'll find, I think, doors open up just by reaching out, having conversations, finding people on LinkedIn. The other thing is to pick up the local business journal. Again, especially in Austin, the Austin Business Journal is loaded with new companies and new things happening every day. So, I would say, get in touch with what's happening in your city.

What does "using sports as a vehicle" mean to you?

To me, that statement would mean that there is an end to everybody's athletic career, whether that ends in college or if you play professional sports. At some point, our bodies are not going to go on forever and allow us to compete at the highest levels. So, I think that it shouldn't be what defines you holistically, but rather, something that can help put you on a path and help play a part of the full 360 degrees of yourself.

A. J. ABRAMS

STATS

SPORTS CAREER:

➤ All time scoring leader in high school

➤ 3X District MVP and 3X District All First team

➤ University of Texas Men's Basketball Team, 2005 - 2009

➤ Big 12 All Freshman team, 2005 - 2006

➤ 120 made 3-pointers set a Big 12 Conference record, 2006 - 2007

➤ All Big 12 second team, 2007 - 2008

➤ All Time Career Leader at Texas in 3-point field goals made

➤ 28th Player in Texas Men's Basketball History to Score 1,000 Career Points

➤ Broke Big 12 Career Record for 3-pointers, 2009

➤ First in UT History in career 3-pointers made, career games played, career minutes played and career points scored during NCAA Tournament

➤ 3rd in UT history in career scoring and career free throw percentage

➤ 6th in UT history career field goals made, 3-point field goal percentage and career steals

➤ 12th in NCAA history in career 3-pointers made

➤ 3rd in NCAA tournament history in career 3-pointers made

➤ Played Professional Basketball, 2009 - 2013

PROFESSIONAL CAREER:

➤ Real Estate Rookie of the Year at JB Goodwin Realtors

➤ Top 40 Agent at JB Goodwin Realtors

➤ Broker and Owner of Supreme 1 Realty

INTERVIEW

What was your first experience for life after sports?

I made a decision my last year in the Czech Republic that I was done, and then I went back to school. I finished up my six hours at UT, got my degree and graduated from college. Everything I did in college was geared towards working with kids. I looked for a job with the State and I got on with DFPS (Department of Family Protective Services), which is an extension of the State geared towards ensuring child safety working at CPS. I did that for, like a cup of coffee, maybe eight or nine months and figured out that it wasn't for me.

In the meantime, I had started studying to get my real estate license because that's what my sister had always talked to me about. She would say, "When you're finished playing, you should get into real estate." I didn't want to do it because I thought it was sales and I didn't want to be in sales. Well, it is sales, but I thought it was more like a super car sales type of job. I looked into it and figured out that I liked it. I left my job at CPS and jumped into real estate.

What was it about real estate that caught your attention?

Well, the business atmosphere behind it, but it still had the athletic sense to it. Pretty much what you put into this is what you're going to get out of it. For me, it just became my new sport. When you're practicing basketball, for example, in high school, you're practicing every day, doing what you're doing, doing what other people are telling you to do, going the extra mile, all without any knowledge of you going to college just yet. You haven't signed on the dotted line. No college has approached you just yet, but you're preparing yourself to go to college. It's the same thing when you're in college. You're doing all the same things that you can, those things that you can control, in hopes of one day being a professional.

And it's the same thing with real estate. You're working every day. Calling people every day in hopes that somebody gives you a call to either help them buy or sell a house. So, for me, it kind of goes hand in hand. The stuff that you do when no one is looking pays off for you big time. You've got to keep doing it day in and day out and be consistent with it.

Was there someone who helped you with your transition from sports into the real world?

My dad's been working for the State for pretty much his whole professional career. He's the one that helped me get on with CPS. But as far as taking that leap of faith and going into a business that's all commission based, I didn't really have a lot of help. My sister was a realtor in Dallas. She kind of guided me through the process of actually getting my license and where to go and what to do and all that aspect of it. Making the transition from the athletic world to the business world can get lonely. If you don't have the drive or enough discipline to figure out, "Okay, well this is what I'm going to do. This is how it's going to work. This is what I need to do day in and day out," I think it can go downhill real fast.

But that's where that basketball or athletic background comes in. You develop that type of discipline to know that, "Okay, I'm doing the little things right. Something big is going to pay off." I didn't really have a huge role model in making sure the transition was successful or not. It was a lot of trial and error. I would ask a lot of questions of people whom I just randomly came across. There wasn't anybody that I could reach out to on a consistent basis that was trying to do what I was trying to do (going from basketball to a commission-based business). I really had no idea about the business. I didn't graduate with a business degree or anything like that, so it was just a whole new world for me.

You get a lot of "no's" all the time in real estate. Over time, you become immune to it, meaning that you see it as, "They don't need you just yet." But there are a lot of failures from when you're making phone calls and people are constantly shooting you down or saying "No, they don't need any help right now." And so again, it goes back to kind of feeling like you're out on an island because you decided to take this step financially. It's a pretty good penny to get into real estate, but, if you're not closing deals, you're not eating. You know what I'm saying? So, if you're not making any transactions, not closing anything, no money is coming in. So, the biggest failure is in not making sure that you have the correct mindset. Most people don't come in with the correct mindset when getting into real estate. To expand on that, most people get into it with the agent mindset, instead of an entrepreneur mindset. If you don't have the entrepreneur mindset, that's where the failure comes in, because you're looking short-term instead of long-term.

You said that you had two different jobs before real estate, right?

I had that CPS job and that was for eight or nine months. Then I took another job in a sales environment to get me prepared for real estate. I was engaged and preparing for the wedding, so I didn't want to jump into real estate at full commission with all the expenditures that a wedding has.

Instead, I left CPS and went to work at a medical recruiting firm, basically recruiting doctors to go work at different hospitals. It's a straight sales job. You're calling different doctors' offices trying to get people on the phone to see if they want to move jobs and things like that.

It's the sales of all sales. We had to make a hundred and fifty phone calls a day. I knew it was temporary, but I still wanted to get a paycheck while preparing for the wedding and to jump into real estate.

That job actually prepared me for two different settings. Since I knew I wasn't going to be there long-term, I really had to kick it in gear and actually get prepared to do real estate. Both jobs actually went hand-in-hand.

People who knew me before real estate knew that I didn't talk a lot. I was super reserved. I still am. That previous sales job taught me how to pick up the phone and just start making random phone calls to people, using my voice to get what I needed in order to actually put some deals together.

In my current profession, you have to be personable. It's allowed me to come out of my shell a little bit. Then when you transition to being self-employed, you're taking on a bigger role because, "You eat what you kill."

If I'm not out there making deals or meeting people, then I'm not bringing money home to my family. It was a big transition for me. I had to accept that I'm probably going to have to change some stuff about myself, because there's no way that I could stay the same and expect different results.

What do you think three benefits of playing sports are?

The very first thing you learn when playing sports is the aspect of hard work. You learn hard work, discipline and time management; especially the higher up that you go. They all go hand-in-hand. You're not just working hard on the athletic field or managing your time for the athletic field. You're managing your time to actually go to college, go to class, practice; things like that. You have to have the discipline to go to the study hall and do what needs to be done. You need to be done so that you can be prepared for practice.

What is one principle that you have learned throughout sports that has helped prepare you for your life today?

My dad would always tell me that if he were to leave this earth right here and now, the only thing he would leave me with is confidence. I've kind of really stuck with that, because I realize that if I'm not confident in what I'm doing, I'm not going to be successful.

And I'm just, I guess, arrogant enough to believe that anything I do, I'm going to be good at it and that's just that confidence aspect of it. I know if I'm confident, I'm going to put some work into it. I'm going to actually go out there and try to be the best at it. I think that's the biggest life principle that I go by.

There are a lot of people that are in whatever field that they're in, and either they don't like it or they're just not confident enough in it to actually go out there and try to be the best at it. And I think that's where I differentiate myself. If I'm going to do it, you're going to know that I'm doing it, because I'm going to make some noise, not by talking, but by my actions, by going out there and trying to be the best that I can be at it.

What would you say to yourself as a high school athlete?

In high school, I didn't go on my senior trip. There were a lot of things that I missed out on because I put basketball and athletics first. I believe that doing that helped me get to where I am. Did I miss out on a lot of social stuff, being with friends and just kind of being a kid? Absolutely. So, if I could go back, I would tell myself, "Basketball will be there. Friends will be there. Put in your work when it's time, but also go be a kid. Don't let it consume you so much to where you're just putting off building relationships, long-lasting relationships."

I really believe that. You've got to do stuff that you may not want to do in order to get where you want to be. I get it. At the same time, if I get to go back and tell my younger self from high school, "Just relax. Basketball will be here. Go have a little bit of fun with your friends as well," that's what I would say.

What do you believe are three key traits that athletes pick up from sports?

Discipline is a really great trait. I think that's why I've been able to be successful in the next field I went into, because I learned discipline early. When it's time to actually go and do the work, whatever it is, you have to have the discipline to start and finish it.

Another trait you learn is to think outside of the box. For example, during an actual game, with so much going on at the same time, you see things others don't and you make adjustments, because you understand the game and the big picture. Whatever field you go into after sports, you still think like an athlete. You're going to learn the ins and outs of that business and start being able to think outside of the box in order to enhance not only the business, but also your personal growth.

Another great trait is learning to listen. I don't know if listening is a trait as much as it is a skill. You have to actually learn how to listen. Coaches sure try to enforce that learning process. Most people don't really listen. Taking this skill or trait and applying it to a new business adventure is critical to your success.

If you will listen, you will learn. You can learn what others have done and put your own spin on it to see if it will fit your personality. Listening, thinking outside of the box, and having enough discipline to actually go out there and do it are keys to your success.

How does playing sports translate to your respective career?

It kind of goes back to, "You eat what you kill." You're preparing yourself for college in high school without even knowing if you're going to college. You're just preparing for it. You haven't got paid just yet when you're in college, but you're working for it so you can become a professional.

It's the same thing when you're in real estate when you're doing all this marketing and advertising and phone calls and talking to people. Until they actually tell you, "Yes, I want the appointment with you and you can come over," and they actually sign on the dotted line to sell their house or to buy that house, you're still not getting paid. But everything that you do is leading up to that payday. And it's literally the same thing in my eyes. It is in the preparation, whether it's for your sport or for your next real estate transaction.

What has been your greatest moment in sports as it relates to the traits that you have talked about?

I'm pretty sure you know this from being a basketball player. I can't remember how many times I was practicing by myself and I walked up to the free throw line and mentally see myself in the game where I'm down two with one second to go. I just got fouled on a three. We need all three to win. There's nobody in the stands. I just see myself in that situation so that when it does come up in a real game, I have already prepared for it.

There were many instances where I would do that, whether I was shooting free throws, coming off a pick-and-roll by myself, just pretending that someone was there, raising up and shooting the ball. And there were many game winners that I hit. I really believe it's because of that practice and preparation leading up to it. There were game winners in high school, game winners in college and game winners in my professional life that were made simply because I put myself in a position to where the moment wasn't too big for me.

To take the perspective off of me, I still think the biggest celebration or celebratory moment for me was in college. It was when we were playing West Virginia and me being a scrawny freshman in the game with ten seconds to go. I don't know why Rick Barnes had that much trust in me, but whatever, I'll take it. West Virginia scores. I get the outlet, take it down and pass the ball to Kenton Paulino with two seconds to go and he hits the game winner. I shouldn't say I don't know why he trusted me. I believe that because I exuded that type of confidence, whether I was a freshman or a senior, I deserved to be in that moment at that point in time and fortunately it paid off.

If you have an athlete come to you for advice, what is your one piece of advice that would help them think beyond being just an athlete?

I think that it really starts with the parents. Whenever I do a speaking engagement, I always try to invite the parents, because it always starts with them. No matter what anybody says to the kids, they're always going to go back and listen to what their parents say. The piece of advice that I would give all of them is to work hard when it's time to work hard, but when the clock is off, just relax. You can only control the things that you can control and you have to put the rest in God's hands. My wife is a coach, and I heard the other day that one of the parents was saying, "I'm doing everything I can to get her a scholarship." The truth is that you can do all you can, but it's not in your hands. You don't have control over this. You can't control if she gets a scholarship or not. You can't control what college scout comes and looks at that. What you can do is control the effort that you put into it in your training process and in the games, and then after that, you've got to leave it alone. There's nothing more that you can do other than the things that you can control.

What are the first three steps that you would advise an athlete on to prepare them to change lanes and to start thinking about life after sports?

Well, I'll tell you the biggest step and it's not going to be in college and it's not going to be in high school. It's going to start whenever you pick up any interest that you do have. I believe that just because you're good at basketball or good at football doesn't mean you're not good at anything else.

The advice that I would give is that everything needs to run parallel. For example, if I'm interested in art, but I'm also interested in basketball, that doesn't mean I have to put my pencil down and focus purely on basketball. We both know basketball is going to end one day. So, when I'm not practicing basketball, I'm also practicing my art. I'm going to put in the same amount of effort that I'm putting into basketball. It goes back to time management. How much time am I going to put into this art? How much time am I going to put into basketball to where I can be good at both of them? And that's the decision that they're going to have to make early on. Even if you don't have an interest just yet, you'll learn more stuff that you're interested in, whether it is in high school or in college. Don't put more weight on just one. The sport will most likely end.

One of the things that I talk about in my book is FTA. I call it a disease that most athletes get once they finish playing. It's called "First Thing Available". People just jump into the first thing available because they don't know what to do. Did you experience FTA? If so, what action steps did you take to get out of it? If not, what did you do to avoid it?

I believe I did when I went to work at CPS. Getting out of college, I wanted to get some type of income as quickly as I could. Since everything that I had done in college was geared towards working with kids, it seemed natural. I realized very quickly that this was not what I wanted. I wanted to try to do something different to create the lifestyle I wanted to have. Fortune favors the bold. So, I took a leap of faith.

What does "using sports as a vehicle" mean to you?

Using sports as a vehicle is a really good term, because it allows you to realize that sports does end. You're just using it as a means to get to where you want to be. I can see how sports hindered me in that

I didn't talk to many people. I had this attitude that if you weren't talking to me about basketball, then I didn't really want to talk to you. A little too focused! But if you really use the college atmosphere and environment for what it's for, you can use all of it as a vehicle, not just a sport. The vehicle is not just to get you where you want to go. It is also about what you are picking up along the way. You are taught life-long traits that increase your ability to succeed in every area of life. And when it's time to crossover, you can. Most employers like the fact that you're a former athlete for those very reasons that I just talked about.

I personally like talking to ex-athletes to see what their mindset is, to see if they want to jump into real estate because they have the attributes that it takes in order to be disciplined enough to be successful in real estate. Are all athletes successful? No, not at all. But they do have the traits that come along with it, or at least they should, if they were successful in that sport. Whatever sport you are in, learn how it can relate to other fields and other careers. That's how you're going to be able to use it as a vehicle to get to where you want to be. The air is going to come out of the ball one day and if you haven't prepared yourself for it, then that vehicle that you were just using is going to run out of gas.

CAT OSTERMAN

STATS

SPORTS CAREER:

➤ The University of Texas Women's Softball Team; 2002-2006

➤ 3x National Player of the Year

➤ 4x All American

➤ 2x Olympic medalist (silver 2008 and gold 2004)

➤ Holds Big 12 Pitching Triple Crown for leading career wins, ERA, strikeouts, as well as shutouts and no hitters.

➤ Claimed the NCAA Division I Records for strikeout ratio.

➤ Named #3 Greatest College Softball Player

➤ Professional Softball Career, 8 years

➤ Part of U.S National Team; 2001 - 2010; 2019

➤ Led UT to 3 Women's College World Series appearances in 2003, 2005, and 2006.

➤ Only individual to win USA Softballs National Player of the Year honors 3 times after earning the honor each of those seasons.

PROFESSIONAL CAREER:

➤ Fifth season as Assistant Coach and second as Associate Head Coach at Texas State.

➤ Serves as pitching coach; 60 shutouts and 157 wins in her four seasons.

➤ Helped reach a 2018 Sun Belt Conference Championship in both the regular season and the tournament.

➤ Coached at DePaul University as Assistant Coach; 2008-2010

➤ 3 straight Big East Championships, 2 NCAA Regional appearances and a 129-50 record

INTERVIEW

What was your first experience for life after sports?

I played professionally for so long, and I did my coaching career simultaneously, so for a while, it was hard for me to say that I had a life after sport because I continued to do both. But I retired in 2015 and went straight into coaching. I can tell you, the first morning I woke up knowing I was done playing, I felt like an 18-wheeler had hit me, both emotionally and physically. It was just all of a sudden, a weight off my shoulders, but at the same time, I felt empty. It was like, "Okay, this is over and done with. What's next?" That first morning after, I felt somewhat lost, not in necessarily a bad sense. I knew I had my job to come to, I knew I still had a career outside of what I had been doing playing. I think for most athletes, it takes up so much our life that when we walk away from it, it takes some time to really comprehend that it's okay to be done playing.

You went basically from college to professional to coaching. Correct?

I knew I always wanted to coach. It's been my desired career path since I was in fourth grade. So, for me, I knew that was what I was going to do. I spent about six years doing both simultaneously. Finally, just cutting off the playing piece, I took some stuff off my plate, which obviously makes you be able to have a little bit more time to yourself. But, at the same time, you sit there wondering, "What do I do next?" Well, it's easy what you do next; you have your job. But for us, we've woken up every day to go train, to go practice, to go with a goal in mind. I think, for the first time, a lot of times when you step away from the game, it's, "What's my goal now?"

What are some examples of how you may have failed before gaining the momentum you have?

That's a tough question. I think going into coaching, everything is a trial and error until you figure out your way. I did it six years simultaneously, but I still don't think I was even very confident in the way I was doing things. It was probably about two and a half years out here at Texas State before I really felt like, "Okay, I know what I'm doing and what I'm doing is working and I should keep going on this route."

Everyone says that great players don't always make great coaches. I have forever wanted to redefine that. I didn't want to be a player that couldn't coach, because I wanted to coach. My heart was in it. I continuously tried to learn and make sure I knew how to relate to people in order to avoid that stereotype.

At the same time, you still have to play trial and error and figure out what it is exactly that's going to make other people tick. It was a solid trial and error and failing for probably a solid two or three years before I really figured out this is the path and this is how I'm going to do it, and be confident in it.

I think it's a funny thing that we're really confident as athletes and as soon as we decide to step outside of our competition, then all of a sudden, we're not so confident. We like what we do, or we know what we're doing, but we're not nearly as confident most times as we are when we're actually playing our sports.

What do you think three benefits of playing sports are?

One is it helps breed confidence. As you get to experience success, and most of us get to experience success at a high level, it does make us extremely confident and capable of facing adversity.

Another benefit is the community you get, whether it's coaches, trainers, teammates, some of those people that we all play with for so long and work with for so long become your mentors, and your guidance, and your circle when you need to hear the truth or when you need advice.

The third is that it teaches you how to work hard.

Athletics is the one thing that you can't pick up a phone and get instant feedback. With athletics you actually have to work at what you want to be good at. I think it teaches people how to work hard, how to work for your goals, and just to let you know there's a process in how all this unfolds. It's not simply, "I want to be good, so, I'm going to be good."

How are you getting from point A to point B? I think sports is one of the last things that teaches that, because you can't get instant feedback or instant answers. You have to fail in order to succeed.

What is one principle that you have learned throughout sports that has helped prepare you for your life today?

I think the biggest principle or quality that sports taught me was a work ethic. I think a lot of people also assume that some of the greatest athletes were always good. If you asked us, obviously, that's not the case. Most of us were not good, or average for a little while. We didn't just pick up whatever ball or equipment that we wanted to play and automatically be deemed one of the greatest athletes.

For me, sports gave me a work ethic where I saw the payoff. It was also rewarding. I loved the work I put in every single day, and so I have tried to take that same work ethic and passion into coaching. Coaching is something I love just as much as playing. That work ethic has been my foundation and pillar in my life.

If I can't go to work every day and give 110%, whether it's for two hours of practice or four hours of practice, then I don't need to be doing this job. For me, it's that work ethic. I want to continue working and learning and that day that I don't want to do that anymore is the day I know I need to find something else to do.

If you could go back and talk to yourself as a college athlete, what would you say to yourself that could help prepare you for life today?

As a college athlete, I think the first thing I would tell myself is that if you eat better, you're going to feel better. I think it's when you say, "What do you know now that you wish you knew then?" I wish the knowledge about nutrition had been stronger while I was in school.

Sitting and eating a whole row of Oreos in one sitting is probably not great; not that I ever thought that was healthy. I think knowing how nutrition can help you recover would have been one of the things that I would have harped on with myself.

I also think I would have told my college self to enjoy it a little more. I wanted to win so bad that I think sometimes I forgot to enjoy the process and the people that I was around. I have my circle of friends that came from our team there at Texas, but in the overall scheme, I probably didn't enjoy my other teammates as much as I should have. I think I would have told my college self to learn how to balance your need and desire to win with being able to relax and have fun and enjoy the moments and not just try to create them and continue on.

What would you say to yourself as a high school athlete?

As a high school athlete, I would tell myself to keep working. To my high school self, I would just continue to encourage myself to trust in the process and to take high school as the experience of how are you going to get better versus winning. I think my dad did a good job knowing that I was at a high school that had just opened and putting that perspective in mind. I took it seriously, but I didn't take it as seriously as I did in college. In college, all I wanted to do was win. Literally, that's all I wanted to do. High school, I did enjoy it a little more.

As a high school athlete, I would tell myself to continue to work, buy into the process, but probably bring some teammates with you. I could probably have helped some teammates out a little bit more than I did and it would have helped us probably in the long run. I may have told myself to engage your teammates a little more and help them, because obviously they weren't as experienced in softball as I was.

What do you believe are three key traits that athletes pick up from sports?

I think athletes learn how to carry and present themselves. It goes a little bit with confidence, but I just think they know how to walk into a room and present themselves, because you walk onto your court or field and you can't walk in with shoulders slumped and look like you're defeated, or else you're not winning that race or you're not playing that game very well.

Sports also give athletes the ability to adapt to others. Obviously not all of your teammates are the exact same personality. No matter what sport you're playing, the people you encounter are all different. For athletes, by the time you decide you're done playing, you're able to communicate, work with and adapt to different kinds of people.

The third trait is they're hard workers, they're grunts workers, they're going to put in the extra work because they know that's what it takes to be elite. Athletes know that you have to work day-to-day. It's not just a once in a blue moon kind of work ethic in order to be successful.

If you have an athlete come to you for advice, what is your one piece of advice that would help them think beyond being just an athlete?

I would tell an athlete to find out what about the sport is your passion. For me, I've been able to realize that my passion was in the pursuit of trying to perfect pitching, which is absolutely impossible. The passion was chasing excellence or chasing to try and get as perfect as possible, and pitching gave me that.

So, how can I put that into my everyday life? Well that's how I approach coaching. I'm never going to be the perfect coach, no one is. You're never going to call the perfect game, or give the right signs, or call the right plays 100% of the time. But what can you do to make yourself as close to perfect as possible?

I think a lot of times an athlete will say, "Oh, my passion is basketball," or, "My passion is soccer." Well, what is it about that? Is it the strategy? If it's the strategy, how can you take that to your life outside of softball or sports? If you can take strategy, okay, maybe you're a better suited for a different career than coaching.

If you just like grunt work, then okay, what grunt work can you do outside of your sport? I think our passion for sports is really rooted in something deeper, and that's what I try to talk to my athletes about. What part of this is your passion? And then, how can we take that into real life? That way we're continuing to be able to live that passion later. I really think we all play sports because we're passionate about it, and not simply just as something to do. You don't play at a high level just because it's something to do.

What are the first three steps that you would advise an athlete on to prepare them to change lanes and to start thinking about life after sports?

To a freshman, I would say step one is to decide. Not to say decide what your endpoint is, but decide where your destination is. Which way are you headed? I think a lot of freshmen come in and think it's, "Yes, we have two years usually to declare a major," and all that, but start to get an idea of what is it that you want to be. Is it a coach? Is it in the medical field? Even if it's broad, find a vague destination of what you want to do. Find yourself a direction. I guess direction would be the better word instead of destination. Find yourself a direction.

Step two, is to put in the work to figure out what traits and characteristics you have that are going to help you get in that direction. The third step would be, "Okay, what aren't you good at that you need to figure out before it's too late in order to continue on your direction."

As a sophomore, I think the first step is obviously you have your direction now. Start to fine tune it little bit, start to hone in on, "Okay, I'm going this direction, my destination should probably be a little bit more specific," but still you don't have to pinpoint, "Okay, I want to be an anesthesiologist." You can see the medical field, or start to get an area of interest.

I think step two now is, "Okay, what things outside of class can I do, or read, or look up in order to help myself be more knowledgeable about what it is I want to do?" I think, unfortunately, there's a lot of us that just think college is going to prepare us, and really, going to history class doesn't help you a whole lot when you want to be in the medical field or in the science field. "What can I start doing outside of class?" Even if it's just reading, do something that helps me start to figure how to make my destination a reality.

Then, the third step, I think as a sophomore, I would encourage kids or athletes, during the little off time that you have, to find a way to get in touch with somebody who is doing what you think you might want to do, even if it's just having conversation. Maybe it's not shadowing them yet, or going and doing internships.

If you have those opportunities, by all means do them, but find someone that's doing what you want to do and start having a conversation so you can get prepared on what it's going to take. Once you know what it's going to take, you can start mapping out your last two years in order to be prepared for that.

I think as a junior is when you really have to obviously hone in, "This is what I want to do." If it's grad school, okay, here's the five grad schools I think I want to go to. If it's a job, okay, here's the five companies I think I need to work for, or I want to work for. I think you obviously hone in right there because, as a senior, once you graduate, it's time to go and take that adventure.

I think step two would be do everything you possibly can to prepare yourself to be knowledgeable about that field, or whatever lane you're going to be crossing into. I think we wait too long a lot of times, as seniors, to start trying to cram it in. And really, if you start preparing as a junior, once you graduate, you're way more confident in the knowledge that it's going to take to be successful in your new lane.

Every free second you have, Christmas break, summer, whatever it is, find a way to read up on what you're doing, go visit people, make cold calls. I think that's the hardest thing for college athletes to do is to get the courage to either cold call, or cold email somebody and just say, "Hey, I'm interested. Would you help me out and answer some questions?" But the more you can get as many perspectives as you can get, the more prepared you're going to be.

Then third, I would start going and visiting people, going and talking to people, find conventions or networks of people, even if it's casual meetings, meetings over coffee, start networking and talking to people that are doing the job you'd like to do.

Then, as a senior, I think the biggest three steps of changing lanes I would say is give it all you got. Leave everything you have on the field or the court. We only get four years to play college, and some people can handle that better than others. If you leave your all out on the court, or the softball field, or the soccer field, then you have no reason to ever look back and say, "What if?"

When you change lanes, you won't hold onto that part of you that's like, "What if I had done this?" Or, "What if I had done that? Could I have had a better career?" You're ready to change lanes because you've left it all there.

The second thing is to be as consumed with your next adventure as you are with sports. Whatever lane you're changing into, whatever job it is, let that consume you as well. You can be consumed by two things at once. You really can. There are going to be two different things, where it's not like you're going be thinking about work while you're playing your sports. You can play your sport, be consumed with that and then, when you go home, be able to start consuming yourself with what your next thing is you are going to do.

Then, the third step I would tell any senior, dive in head first. Put your whole heart out there and go make it what you want it to be. I think too many of them try to tiptoe in, and if you get an internship, go all in. Be present every day. Be there. Tell them, "What do you want me to do? Okay, I did that. What's next?" Be the one who wants to continue to be hungry, because the sooner you get completely immersed, you're probably going to succeed faster than anybody who just tiptoes in and stays in the background.

What does "using sports as a vehicle" mean to you?

I think using sports as a vehicle means that you get everything you can out of sports. You don't just see it as a physical act of playing your sport. You use sports to better yourself as a person, to prepare yourself for the future, whether that's tomorrow or ten years down the road.

Sports can teach you so many things if you're open to it. I think there are athletes that simply play the sport and don't want to look past the Xs and Os of the sport, and in that case it's not really a vehicle for them, it's a means to an end.

But if you're going to use sports as a vehicle, you're open to letting it transform you and letting it teach you more than just, "Oh, I didn't make that shot," or, "I didn't get that hit," but, "Okay, I didn't make that shot. How am I going to bounce back next time I'm in that situation?" You let sports change you and make you, kind of mold you, as opposed to just using it as something you're doing.

MARK HENRY

STATS

SPORTS CAREER:

➤ An American Powerlifter, Olympic Weightlifter, Strongman and Retired Professional Wrestler

➤ 2X Olympian; gold, silver, and bronze medalist at the Pan American Games.

➤ Powerlifter World Champion and 2X U.S. National Champion and All-Time Raw World Recordholder in the squat, deadlift and total and the USA Powerlifting American Record in deadlift

➤ Credited for the biggest raw powerlifting total ever performed by a drug-tested athlete, regardless of weight class, as well as the greatest raw deadlift by an American citizen.

➤ Weightlifting 6X U.S. National Weightlifting Champion, an American Open Winner, a 2X U.S. Olympic Festival Champion and a NACAC Champion

➤ Holds all 3 Senior US American Weightlifting Records of 1993 - 1997

➤ Won First Annual Arnold Strongman Classic, 2002

➤ WWE 1X Champion and 2X World Champion

➤ World Heavyweight Championship, 2011

PROFESSIONAL CAREER:

➤ Mentor and Speaker

➤ Current Sirus XM Radio Host

➤ Actor in movies and television

➤ Super Dad

INTERVIEW

What was your first experience for life after sports?

Well, I really have not completely been out, but my experience after sports has been going and mentoring and speaking, doing a lot of speaking engagements. I work in talent development for the WWE, whom I have worked for the last 23 years.

I've also started doing radio on Sirius XM, where I have a show called "Busted Open." We talk about pro-wrestling. And now, a few acting gigs. I'm moving forward in that world too.

What made you go in that direction as far as mentorship? What guided you to that?

I've been fortunate enough to have a bunch of really, really smart people around me. I had a lot of people help me along the way. There's no way that I would have become who I became if I didn't have these certain individuals giving me good direction and holding me to a high standard; forcing me, basically, to live up to their expectations, as well as mine.

What are some examples of how you may have failed before gaining the momentum you have?

In my career, I've competed so many times that I can't remember all the wins and losses, nor do I really focus on them. I've won more than I have lost. I know that for sure. When I lost, I was a horrible loser. Still, I'm really not good to be around when I lose. I sulk, I pout, I get very short, and I start thinking immediately about how I can better myself, so that I can beat this person next time or I can beat this situation again.

As it relates to pro wrestling, it's more entertainment than competition, so I just wanted to have the best performance on the show. I used to really revel in the fact that I had a good performance and people had to follow me. Like, yeah, good luck with that.

When I was in powerlifting, I only had one loss in my career and it was at the World Championships or at the National Championships. I was 18 and everybody else was much older. I was the youngest competitor in the field and I came in second. I was just like, "Man, I'm never going to lose again," and I never did in that sport.

I moved on to Olympic weightlifting and nine months of training and I made the Olympic team. Twelve months a year of training, I came in 10th place at the Olympic games in 1992. After that, I never lost again in the United States. I won everything except the Olympic games, and I suffered an injury in Atlanta, Georgia in 1996 and I was having the best competition of my life.

I mean, it just really hurt and I didn't think that the Olympic Committee at the time was making the rules better suited for somebody that was not taking steroids. Because I was not taking drugs, I took every opportunity I could to complain about people I was competing against who were taking drugs. I'm a horrible loser and I'm the type that's not going to sleep well until I win again.

What do you think three benefits of playing sports are?

I think that confidence is a definite benefit. I think of my experiences from growing up in my little town of Silsbee to coming to Austin, going to Colorado Springs, to the Olympic Training Center, coming back to Austin, going to New York and to all my travels around the world. Confidence just makes you feel like you're somebody.

The next benefit is the exposure to the world. Sports have done so much for me. It allowed me to be able to feed my family, to travel the world, to expose myself to people that I would not have met otherwise. I've been to the White House, to the British Parliament. I've been to so many residences of powerful people and kings and queens and palaces and stuff that you would only read about, and it was all because of sports. I paid attention and sports introduced me to all these people and places.

Another benefit is the feeling of accomplishment. I didn't waste my time and I didn't waste my life. I did what no other human being has been able to do and that's to be somebody, to be the strongest person that ever lived and to compete in three different, well, four different sports and win a World Championship in three of the four. I feel very accomplished.

What is one principle that you have learned throughout sports that has helped prepare you for your life today?

One principle is respect. I respect the work that I do and I respect the people that helped me with my work. I am respectful of other people's time because people could be doing something else.

What do you believe are three key traits that athletes pick up from sports?

The competitive nature is something I think you take with you for the rest of your life. Once you are a competitor, you always want to be competitive. Another trait would be that you don't want to regress. You don't want to take a step down to something or someone or somewhere because where you've been has been so educational and you're appreciative of what you have attained. You kind of get spoiled.

As athletes, you get treated differently according to whether you win or lose, so you want to win. You want to keep going up. I have maintained a high priority trait for me and that is to be on time. If we say 11:00, it means 11:00 to me or it means 10:50. It has stuck with me the most and I've had people tell me, "Oh, man, you're on time." They are amazed that I'm on time. I have heard people say often that others are never on time. I'm like, "Wow, really?"

Is there any other reason why you chose wrestling and powerlifting?

As a kid, I just felt strong. Powerlifting was natural to me. All my childhood photos are of me flexing. In the fourth grade, I went to a Halloween party as the Incredible Hulk. My mother used a wash off paint, painted me green, tore my clothes all up and I was the Hulk because that's how I felt.

Being with my grandmother, she just got me addicted to watching wrestling. After the Olympics, I was on Oprah and a bunch of other shows, and I said that I was a wrestling fan. Then the WWE basically reached out to me.

If you have an athlete come to you for advice, what is your one piece of advice that would help them think beyond being just an athlete?

There are many things that a person can do to help other people in their lives beyond being just an athlete. You can help elevate their thinking to the point where it will even help their kids, and their kid's kids. If you are successful, you have an even greater opportunity to help others. I feel it's our duty as successful people to try to not leave it or take it to the grave with you.

I always remember my mother was very giving. My manager, who ended up being like my dad, did for others all the time, so I had good examples. I was also able to see how other people were so giving to people they didn't even know, to strangers. They didn't have to help me like they did, but they did and I'm very appreciative for it.

What does "using sports as a vehicle" mean to you?

To find something that you can elevate your life with. There have been places that I've wanted to go, but how do I get there? Sometimes, you've got to be able to put your pride aside and call somebody and say, "Hey, man, you're in this field, would you happen to know anything about this?" Or, "Excuse me, Ma'am, I don't know much about this, but I think that I heard you say something about it before."

It's better to go ask somebody that will know more than you and realize that you don't know every damn thing. Like, I mean, I've been exposed to the world, I know a lot about a lot of things, but I don't know everything and shouldn't be expected to know everything. At least I know that there's room for growing, room for knowing, and it's just going to take work and it's going to take putting your pride aside and asking for help sometimes.

__What are the first three steps that you would advise an athlete on to__
__prepare them to change lanes and to start thinking about life after sports?__

Number one, to start now preparing for the end, because the end is inevitable. Father-time is undefeated. You're going to have to step away from whatever it is you're doing one of these days, especially if you're using your body, because the body is going to weaken as you get older.

Preparation for the future will be number one and number two, to be realistic with yourself and to not waste your time on pipe dreams, but find something concrete that you're good at, that you like to do.

Sometimes, you can get in a field where it doesn't even feel like work. You would do it anyway. I remember my mother told me I was being a clown. I can't even remember what I did, but she said, "I wish you could make some money acting a damn fool." It was very fortunate that I ended up making money acting like a damn fool!

If you do what you love, then you don't feel like you ever worked a day in your life. You would just do it anyway and that's kind of where I am. I'm hustling and I get tired. I'm tired now, but what else am I going to do with my time but work? I just ... golly, I don't know. I'm not the sit and watch the grass grow type of dude.

Lastly, just to have pride and to want to do good. Like, just want to be somebody, just want to accomplish something. Wake up with something in mind to get done. I will go and educate myself more about something I don't know about. Something. Become more. Get better trained at something that you already do. Keep learning. You can never really get too educated or polished if you have that mindset.

__In your profession, can you tell the difference in people who have played sports before and the ones who didn't? If so, what is that difference?__

Not always, but for the most part, you find athletes wanting to make a competition out of stuff that doesn't even require being competitive. I mean, I've been walking by a garbage can and threw something at it and missed. It ended up becoming a competition between somebody who saw me miss. "Aw, you missed that short shot?" "Well, you come do it." Then, you end up shooting at a basket or a garbage can. It's insane. That's what you find from an athlete, that kind of competitive nature. Throwing darts is another one. Anything.

Chapter 12

INTERVIEWS WITH COACHES

COACH CATHY SELF MORGAN

COACH KEELEY HAGAN

COACH KRYSTAL ELLIS

COACH JEAN-PAUL HEBERT

COACH KAREN ASTON

COACH CATHY SELF MORGAN

STATS

➤ TABC Hall of Fame, 2017

➤ TAGC Hall of Fame, 2018

➤ High School Basketball (Gatorade Coach of the Year)

➤ Won more than 1,000 career games and eight state titles combined between Austin, Westlake and Duncanville.

➤ Duncanville Head Coach; 2000 – Current

➤ Led teams to eight state championships - three at Westlake and five at Duncanville.

➤ Inducted into Texas Sports Hall of Fame, 2018.

➤ 2017 Gatorade Coaching Excellence Award.

➤ 2014 named National High School Girls Basketball Naismith Coach of the Year and Women's Basketball Coaches Association Coach of the Year

➤ Selected to coach McDonalds All American All Star Game, 2004 and 2010

➤ Selected to be one of the head coaches for the Jordan Brand Classic, 2017

INTERVIEW

What do you believe are at least three benefits of playing sports?

One is for young ladies to be a part of something that is bigger than themselves, for them to be a part of the team and learn their roles in helping that team be successful. It also helps them learn to be a part of a family that all gives and takes and learns to love each other. It helps them develop their self-confidence and their self-esteem. It's going to help them in roles outside of playing in that sport.

What is one principle that you would like for athletes to take away from sports?

It would be in understanding how to be a part of a successful team. And how important it is that everybody has their role. Everybody contributes and everybody cares and has each other's back and loves each other.

How can sports help athletes in school?

Again, it goes to the self-esteem and confidence. They develop through sports something good about themselves. You know, actually looking good, because they're staying in shape, and they're working at it, and that's going to help them feel good about themselves too.

It also helps them to follow through and to finish projects. To prepare ahead of time and learn to study and then bring their brain cells every single day to class, because you've got to do that same thing in your sports. And I think it's a good, strong carryover into learning to be successful.

What is your one piece of advice to an athlete that would help them think beyond being just an athlete?

I would tell them that there's more to life. You can just be an athlete, but you can also be someone's daughter, someone's friend, someday somebody's mother. And you're going to have to take care of all facets of life to survive and take care of yourself, and be independent, and self-sufficient.

What do you believe are three key traits that athletes pick up from sports?

Grit, working hard to stay with something and not giving up. Sometimes learning to deal with failure and how to turn that into success. Learning to be strong and self-sufficient. Grit is when you go after something with everything you've got and you do it continually. You persevere through thick and thin, through things that are hard and you still just push through. You give it your all. It's the loose balls; it's the finish; it's the supporting each other when you're on the bench. Grit, to me, is just that desire to be the best you can be and nothing less, even if you do have to deal with failure. And again, how you're going to turn that into being the best you can be.

How does playing sports translate to your respective career?

That there has to be a plan, and there has to be a process. You know, my plan starts with elementary kids being involved in basketball. The process is where we all work together for the same thing. I've got 10 coaches on my staff and they know what the program is. They're all pushing to follow through with that.

But at the same time, we're trying to help the young ladies learn to have fun and enjoy what they're doing. And when they have tough things going on in their life, to put those problems up on a shelf, and come in, and just play the sport, enjoy it. And then go back and work on that problem after you've given your all in whatever we were doing that day.

What does "using sports as a vehicle" mean to you?

Everybody wants to get somewhere. In sports, we talk about setting goals. We set goals in seventh grade. I'm sure that parents set goals for their children even when they're younger. I mean, I always did with my daughter.

When you have that goal, you've got to have what you're calling a vehicle to get there. I call it a process. And, you're going to go through a lot of trials and tribulations to get there. You're going to have flat tires. You're going to have to back up. You're going to have to go forward.

It's like I say, this weekend we didn't play well at all, it's like we took two steps forward and one step back. And that's where your vehicle is. You've got to just keep on pushing through using that grit, with that perseverance, with that determination.

My process is still unfolding. I'm not there yet. I'm 63 years old, and I still am not where I want to be. I know I'm going to get there, so I'm still driving that car. Too often in that left lane, I'm going too fast, but I push through to get to what I need in order to get done.

Is there anything else that you would like to add?

Yes. Young ladies and people need to not be afraid to ask questions and to ask for help. Go to people. When I came here to Duncanville, I went to our head football coach. He was successful. Our head baseball coach was successful. Even when I was a college player, I called Sandra Meadows, who was a legend here in Duncanville in coaching. I went to watch Pat Summitt's practices and picked her brain.

And, that young ladies need to reach out and not be afraid to reach out. We don't have to do things alone. There are always people that have had experience in doing it and you can talk to them. We can reach out. People are always willing to help. Help you grow, and help you get better. I would like to add that Ashley Roberts is writing this book. She's on a good course and doing a great job with it, and she's not afraid to go out there and talk to people and ask them questions, ask for guidance.

COACH KEELEY HAGEN

STATS

COACHING

- Assistant Coach, 10 Years (Four at University of Tennessee and six at The University of Texas)
- Coach and played at University of Tennessee
- Helped lead Texas to 61 victories, a pair of Big 12 Championship Semifinal berths, and two NCAA Tournament berths, including a Sweet Sixteen in 2017

PLAYER

- 3x National All American, Sec Defensive Player of the Year; 2004
- U-19 & U-21 National Team
- Professional soccer (two years in Sweden; two in US)
- Women's Professional Soccer (WPS) Championship with Sky Blue FC; 2009
- US Women's National Team Pool; 2008-2009

INTERVIEW

What do you believe are at least three benefits of playing sports?

They are challenged into being pushed out of their comfort zone. Part of that challenge is that their character gets challenged. They get challenged in their relationships under stress, whether it's individual stress or team stress. The sport gives them the benefit of going through adversity. Learning how to deal with failure and adversity and how to get past that and move forward.

What is one principle that you would like for athletes to take away from sports?

I think the biggest thing is just pursuing the best version of themselves. Sports reveal a lot, especially during adversity and sports reveals character. It's really just pushing to become the best version of themselves and not comparing themselves to other people and always pushing and striving to be better and not average.

How can sports help athletes in school?

Sports teaches athletes many things that translate to school and life. It teaches responsibility for yourself, doing your role in your sport and for your teammates, putting their needs above yours first. Bringing the right equipment, coming prepared and on time. Paying attention to the details. Making the right runs, touching the line.

The details matter in sport and in school. It teaches you teamwork and working together with your teammates in different environments.

You need to learn how to work with your classmates. It teaches you structure and time management.

A clear structure provides boundaries necessary to stay on task to work towards a common goal. School is structured to have you do the same. Time management is crucial to get the things done you want and need to get done.

What is your one piece of advice to an athlete that would help them think beyond being just an athlete?

Well, being an athlete obviously helps with a ton of things in the real world, but it can't define you. It can't be your identity. That would be the biggest thing. Too many people wrap themselves up in their sport and that's who they are. You have to know who you are outside of your sport. Don't let your sport be your identity.

Why do you enjoy coaching your athletes and helping to keep them involved in sports?

I enjoy just seeing the growth of the individual. You come in as a freshman and you have this idea of what things are going to be like. You really just don't have any idea at all. Especially when it comes to the game in terms of the intensity, the expectations, and the demands. I think most people would think it's a pretty big jump from high school to college, especially if you're playing at a high level in college. So, it's really cool for me to see the development, particularly off the field, from their freshman year to their senior year and just how much they mature as a human being.

The core principles that we're teaching are principles that are going to carry them through life. And it's the littlest thing, from, "Hey, put your foot behind the line, not on the line." You don't cut corners at all and you know you're giving your teammates energy. It's pretty neat to see a freshman come in who has not really been taught those things. By the end of it, they're the senior that's leading the team and influencing other people to do those things that you've taught and instilled in them.

What does "using sports as a vehicle" mean to you?

As an athlete, they can use sports as a platform after college to drive them and get them to where they want to go with those experiences that they've gone through. So literally when you say vehicle, it's like they can use these experiences however they want. And for those who will take the most advantage of their four years in college and use as many resources as the college provides (whether that's your professors or the community service resources we have here, the coaches or people or whatever), that's just going to open so many more doors for them after school.

How does being a former athlete translate to what you do as a coach?

I definitely think it's a big factor. You are who you are because of your examples. You learn from them. Either I'm going to make a decision to go this way because of this experience or go another way. I've always been taught that every choice is an important choice, as small as that choice might be. I think my players would say this as well. I'm really demanding because that's how I was as a player on myself. I wanted to make sure that I could control the controllable and work harder than anybody.

And I might not have been the most talented, but I knew that I was going to be more prepared and I was going to outwork my opponents and my teammates. I think that's definitely a big part of how I coach and accountability is such a big thing. I think there's great value in showing people, especially on film, where they messed up. Well, that's okay, because we're here to help you become better and we're going to take a look at it. We're going to keep you accountable and now we're going to move forward from it and just be better.

And ultimately, your positivity and your energy, and always believing that as a player you could do anything because you were prepared and worked hard, will be what causes you to get back up. Just because you knocked me down doesn't mean I was going to stay down. I was going to keep getting back up. I think those are really important key attributes that your team has to have, especially when things aren't going your way.

I would say one of the biggest things I'm learning as a coach, is to understand and be a little bit more empathetic for players that aren't like me. And, how I can meet them where they are in their process to become the best version of themselves. At the end of the day, a great athlete and teammate is going to do those core values that we talked about and they're going to have respect for themselves and their teammates.

They're going to be accountable; they're going to keep their teammates accountable. They've got to have a tough mentality and they're trying to get better every single day with a positive attitude and energy, and they're giving to their teammates and their disciplined in their execution. It's a lot and that's why not everybody can do it, because it's tough. I went through this as a player, because I wanted to be the best that I could be every day. It wasn't just sometimes.

COACH KRYSTAL ELLIS

STATS

- High School Volleyball Coach
- Dallas ISD Rotary Service Above-Self Teacher of the Year, 2017
- Duncanville High School Teacher of the Year, 2008
- Teaching (English, AVID, and Partner PE), 15 years
- Coaching in Public Education (2 years middle school, 13 years high school)
- Coaching Competitive Club Volleyball, 15 years
- Coached over 20 1st place finishes in those 15 years, as well as winning Lone Star (Huge Tournament)
- Head Coaching Experience & Head Coach by age 30, 7 years
- AVID Coordinator (Advancement Via Individual Determination) 6 years; helped over 200 students get to college and over half receive full scholarships and/or aid.
- Hosted the Dallas Volleyball Spring League for 5 years and the Duncanville Tournament of Champions
- Coached 15+ girls who went on to play in college

INTERVIEW

What do you believe are at least three benefits of playing sports?

Number one is social ability and being able to be a people-person and meet and talk to people more easily than maybe an average, everyday kid, especially if you play something like club volleyball or AAU. A regular student goes through life and only sees the teachers they have or the people they see in their classroom, whereas a student that is in athletics will see double that.

For example, if I play school ball, I only interact for four years, sometimes six (if you do middle school), and if you play club or AAU, you double that, so that's 12 years of an opportunity that some get zero of, so they get more interaction with people, which in turn makes them more social and a little bit more extroverted. Also, let's say they go to a tryout. They automatically have to meet new people, so it makes them more personable and able to meet people easier. That's number one.

Number two benefit would be the ability to work with others. No matter what sport you're doing, you always have to work with somebody. You heard your coaches say and you may say, "You don't have to be best friends, but you have to be able to respect each on the court," and so I think that's such a marketable trait, because at any time, you have to be able to work with somebody else.

A lot of people, especially now with social media and everything else, they are becoming more introverted and they're used to talking on the phone, texting, things like that, whereas people who are in sports, they have that face-to-face interaction daily. If I have to work with someone in sports, and solve problems together or work together to reach a common goal, which is winning, then it makes me understand the importance of working with others as a whole.

Number three benefit would be they know the value of hard work, so their work ethic is going to be better than your typical person, because they have to put in the time and effort every day in practice. I should add time management; that's part of it, too. You get so many more opportunities to show your work ethic, because you have to be at every practice. You can't be late. If you are, there's a consequence.

Just like when you go to work, what happens? If you don't show up, you get fired or you get written up. It's the same thing with athletics. You may have gotten an internship, you know you better be on time, because coach told you, "You better be there or else there's going to be a consequence." Working day in and day out and giving your team, your coach, and yourself everything you've got helps you develop a strong work ethic. This becomes a habit, so your expectation becomes to be nothing but the best every single day.

What is one principle that you would like for athletes to take away from sports?

One thing that I want athletes to take away from sports is just the love and respect for the game and for people. We're not all the same, but we come together because we love this sport, and so that gives us something in common. The takeaway is that we ought to love that sport no matter what our differences are. Because of that sport, it brought us together. When you stop loving the game, everything you have put into it starts to falter and it just isn't the same anymore.

How can sports help athletes in school?

You have to pass to play. And, it keeps you focused, especially with volleyball players. We always say the volleyball players are the smart kids, but they just get motivated. In competition in sports, you get competitive, so they compete not only athletically, but also academically. They'll be like, "Hey, Coach, we have to make sure we have a tutorial today. Can we go ahead and take an hour break and come back for an hour afterwards or whatever?" My kids actually begged me to do that.

Because of their work ethic, they just know the value of the academics. They know they have to pass, but then they also know they have to put in the work to do it because of the work ethics they've had from athletics. So, sports help kids be competitive in life, stay focused, and they know the expectations of themselves and how to reach goals.

What do you believe are three key traits that athletes pick up from sports?

A strong work ethic. Kids in sports know that you can't get anywhere in life without a strong work ethic. All the time they put into their skill set and the energy they put into practices, shows them the value of giving everything you've got. As a coach, seeing a kid surpass everything and give all they've got, shows their love of the game and their pride in themselves. They don't run a spring and stop before the line, they learn to run through the line, making them know what it takes to go that extra step, and how important it is.

Time management is another trait. Being an athlete is a tough job. You have to balance home life, school work, social life, sports, and whatever other obligations you have. You spend so much time in class and on the court, and things become prioritized. They understand the importance of being on time, which is really 15 minutes early.

An athlete will be the one at that interview that is there and ready 30 minutes ahead of time. This in turn, helps with discipline and communication, because if they will be late, they learn to let you know and/or there are consequences.

The other is teamwork. Being a part of a team, spending time with your teammates, day in and day out, help athletes know how to work with others. They may not get along day in and day out, but they realize that if you give everything you've got to your team, you will be successful.

You spend a lot of time with your teammates, so they learn how to work together and get a job done. Setting a goal and reaching it, winning a championship together; that feeling is like no other. All that hard work and time you put in with this group of people, it's priceless.

What do you think is an advantage that student athletes have over students who do not participate in sports?

That constant drive, the coach checking on them, always making sure that they got their grades, because otherwise, there are consequences, not only from not playing, but also coaches and having that constant eye over you. Just a regular kid, they don't necessarily have that until the value of education and the value of everything steps up, because you got that person always on your back.

Also, it would have to be confidence. For me, going from places like Duncanville, seeing the basketball program versus the volleyball program and then going to the Dallas ISD program, there's one thing that's been the same. It's a kid's confidence level.

I had no idea that kids' self-esteem was so low until I started working with kids in sports and then saw the difference between the Dallas ISD kids and the Duncanville kids and the club kids. Just because you love the game doesn't mean that you have the confidence to play it.

When I was at Dallas ISD, I wanted to get my Bryan Adams kids through the season knowing enough about the sport that if they went to college and wanted to join an intramural team, they would feel confident enough to do it. Or, if they were playing beach ball out in the backyard or whatever at college or at a company picnic, that they could step in there and confidently play.

I wanted them to believe in themselves enough to put themselves on the court and be able to put themselves out there in society. When you love something and learn more about it, you get the confidence to step in and do the best you can, and possibly even become a leader in it. Confidence builds character, and in turn, helps people believe in themselves.

What does "using sports as a vehicle" mean to you?

To me, it means using it as a leg. When you go somewhere, you gotta get in a vehicle to go somewhere, so sports is that way, that avenue, to get you where you need to go.

COACH JEAN-PAUL HEBERT

STATS

- ➤ Assistant Men's Golf
- ➤ 5 years has helped assist 14 team victories, nine medalist honors, back to back
- ➤ Big 12 championships, 2013 and 2014
- ➤ NCAA championship, 2012
- ➤ Played for University of Texas, 1991 - 1994.
- ➤ 3x All American Men's Golf UT,
- ➤ NCAA champions, 2012
- ➤ Big 12 Conference 5 years in a row, 2013 - 2017
- ➤ Finalist for Assistant Coach of the Year (Jan Strickland Assistant Coach of the year), 2016 - 2017
- ➤ Played Professional Golf, 1995 - 2003

INTERVIEW

What do you believe are at least three benefits of playing sports?

It helps us build relationships with people. There's a great social benefit to sports. We're around people. We're forced to develop competitive-type relationships with people. And we're exposed to people we otherwise may not have been exposed to. It puts us in challenging situations where we can be stronger, we can overcome more, we can be tougher than we would have been maybe without sports.

Through sports, we're able to experience things that we would not have been able to. Maybe we travel to some places that we wouldn't have traveled to. Maybe we get out of a certain town or a certain area that we're used to, and we get to see more of the world.

What is one principle that you would like for athletes to take away from sports?

Learning how to not quit. I think that's a great principle. A great value in life is when you don't give up when things are not really going your way. When things don't look like they are working out for you individually, you just don't quit. You're playing for much more than just yourself, and you learn how to keep on going and keep fighting.

Whether you are having success, or whether you're not having success, you've always got something to compete for, you've always got something to play for. And you just can't quit because you just never know what can happen.

What is your one piece of advice to an athlete that would help them think beyond being just an athlete?

I am always wanting them to think as themselves as more than an athlete. I don't want them to believe that their sport is what makes them who they are. You don't want to be defined by your sport or by a certain achievement. There are many, bigger, more defining moments that will come in their lives. So, it's something that I believe in anyway. And, I always want them to have one eye towards the future. Sometimes, we can point out to a certain analogy or a certain example where, hey look, one of these days you're going to be in this situation. I just want them to think about a bigger picture, and how they can handle something in the future when they're out there on their own.

When they're coaching, or when they're here, and they're a student athlete, they're pretty well taken care of. We do a lot of things for them. And I told them, when you get out in the real world, you have about three people that are going to care for you; your mom, your dad, your sister. Everybody else is going to care for you when it's convenient for them to care for you. So, I want them to understand that there's going to come a time when it's going to be tough, and they are going to have to be tough and deal with life face on.

What do you believe are three key traits that athletes pick up from sports?

I think they pick up respect for other people. You have to learn how to have respect. Respect for your sport, respect for how difficult it is to succeed, to win. I think that sports can be pretty humbling in that respect. They hopefully will learn about integrity, and about what's right, how to do things, play by the rules, and when you're competing, you're trying to win, but there's a right way and wrong way to go about doing things. Play within the rules. You don't want to be known as a cheater, because once you're a cheater, you're always a cheater. And, that's just not how you want to go about the rest of your life anyway.

Respect, integrity, and trying to do something really well. Take pride in your body of work as a student athlete. Do things well or don't waste your time. I think that no matter what it is you're trying to do, try to do a good job. Whether you win or not, try to do a good job, and take some pride in what you're trying to do.

Can you give me some examples of how your team used any of the traits that you mentioned?

Well, our players, they're student athletes. And I think that typically they're more focused on their sport than they are the school side of things, but I really want them to. When it comes to doing things well, taking pride in what you're doing, I want them to take pride in everything that they're doing, including school. I don't expect them to make all A's, I don't expect them to be great students, but I expect them to achieve some level of success in school as well as in their sport.

They're going to have to balance more than just one thing when they get out of school. They're going to have to take on more responsibilities than just their sport. They're going to have some bills, they're going to have relationships, they're going to have a job, they're going to have hobbies, they may have a family, they may have a car payment, they may have a house. They're going to have to juggle and deal with life. So, learn how to handle all those different things instead of just being so single-minded in your life.

And I think that a lot of times when we are in public, and we're a team, we try to make sure that they are representing themselves, and they're representing our school in the right way. When we travel, we don't have a strict dress code, but we have some rules about what they wear on an airplane or when we go to dinner. When we go inside, we take our hats off. When we go to a decent dinner, we actually take our phones and hand them over and put them under the table, and we actually have a meal, and we talk. We build a greater bond among the group. So little things like that we can do to just create some different levels of respect and bonding with our people, and learn how to connect with other people in a different way that maybe they haven't in the past.

They need to be aware of the way they look, and their body language, and their posture, and be aware of what they're doing in their surroundings. Some little kid may be sitting right there, and you understand that you're in public, be careful what you say and how you say it. That maybe some little five-year-old kid's sitting right there. And they see you, and they see our school, or your sports brand right on your sleeve. Well, that's going to matter. It makes a big difference. Last time we did that, we were walking out of there and one of the players says, "We should do that more often." "Yeah, yeah, no worries. We will."

What does "using sports as a vehicle" mean to you?

It means that a sport is going to help one athlete get from this place in their life to hopefully a much better, healthier place in their life. Through sports they can learn, they can achieve, they can develop, they can evolve, they can become more capable and prepared to take on some bigger challenges in life. And they can become more exposed, more experienced, and they can be much more … and they need to be more than their sport.

Maybe there's a rare small percentage of people out there who are so great at what they do that it's truly what defines them, but still we're capable of doing more than just participating in a sport.

Did you always know that you wanted to be a coach even when playing?

No. I didn't. I always appreciated my coaches and I always got along with my coaches. I don't think I really saw myself doing that. I ended up coming back around full circle and I'm back into it. It just naturally happened. When I coach, I'm looking at things from a player's perspective. I remember very clearly what it's like to be a student athlete, to be challenged, to be dealing with all the things we deal with. I just believe in trying to help create an environment for them to succeed in and help them when they need some help and kick them in the butt when they need a little bit of that too.

What did you think you wanted to do coming out of college?

I was interested in being a professional athlete, and I was for about eight years. I played golf on a professional level. I was also interested in entertainment television. I never saw myself as really ending up being a coach. I went full circle, and all the way back around to where I was just naturally involved with our team again. And I started becoming more involved. I enjoyed the relationships that we had with the players. I think I'm a better coach than I was a player actually, because I feel like I've got a very clear picture of what they're going through.

How does being a former athlete translate to what you do as a coach?
Consider your coaching style, how you treat your players, the things
that you do, how you act as a coach.

Well, I think it's a big part of it. There are maybe some coaches out there that actually didn't compete directly in that same sport. They might have crossed over from another sport. I think about my experiences in competition and what might have motivated me, what I might have feared as a competitor, what my motivations were, the different scenarios in which I was in as a competitor, and I think about that.

These athletes are all different, and there's no telling what could be going through their minds. So as a coach, I'm sensitive to that. My style, because of that, is that I'm going to err on the side of coaching less as opposed to over coaching, and I'm going to pay attention, and I'm going to gain a very good understanding of them before I start digging into them.

My style starts with wanting to understand them as people, as competitors, and as athletes. I wanted to figure some things out on my own out there. I want to let my own instincts take over as much as possible, and that's what I want them to do. I want their instincts, and their senses, and their styles, and their natural abilities to play out as much as possible on their own. So, I think I'm a patient coach because of that. And I think that I'm ready to jump in when the times right, but not too soon.

COACH KAREN ASTON

STATS

➤ Associate Head Coach at Baylor University

➤ Associate Head Coach at The University of Texas at Austin, eight seasons

➤ Assistant Coach at University of North Texas, 1996 - 1998

➤ Head Coach at Charlotte University, 2007 - 2011; five consecutive post season appearances, WNIT berth in 2007 - 2008 led to Atlantic 10 Conference Tournament Title and an 11th Seed in the 2009 NCAA Women's Division Basketball Tournament.

➤ Trip to Final Four in WNIT, 2011

➤ Head Coach at University of North Texas, 2011 - 2012; tripled win total first year;

➤ 2012 earned 100th victory as Head Coach.

➤ Head Coach at University of Texas (2012 - current), 3 Sweet Sixteen appearances, 1 Elite Eight appearance.

➤ Big 12 Coach of the Year, 2016 – 2017

➤ Finalist Naismith Coach of the Year, 2016 – 2017

➤ NCAA Final Four, 2003; Associate Head Coach

➤ Big 12 tournament champions; Associate Head Coach

➤ Big 12 regular season champions, 2003; 2004 Associate Head Coach

➤ Atlantic 10 Champions, 2009,

➤ Set a school record for wins in a season at Charlotte University (27), 2010 - 2011

➤ University of Arkansas Girls Basketball Coach of the Year, 1993

INTERVIEW

What do you believe are at least three benefits of playing sports?

I think one benefit is discipline. I think just a daily routine of self-discipline. If you're really, really good at sports, you do have a certain amount of self-discipline. Then, also what is gifted to you from whoever your coach is or whatever the organization is that you're a part of, since most teams have discipline.

On a team sport, another benefit is that perfect word of being a team. I think that any time that you are involved in something that creates a mindset that there's something bigger than you, and you have acquired some selfless behavior, then you're benefiting enormously. I also think that it's just a value that you learn about what it takes to be successful, especially if you're going to be in an organization as you move along in your life. If you're involved in a company that involves teamwork, then I think sports is a great avenue for that.

As I look back on my own experiences as an athlete and then I look at other people that I coach, one of the biggest values of being in athletics is the self-value that you get from it. There's a self-confidence that comes from women in sports that is really, really evident. It may not be actually evident when you first start to see them, but as they grow along in whatever sport they choose to be in, I definitely think that there is a self-worth and a self-confidence that comes from being in sports.

What is one principle that you would like for athletes to take away from sports?

There are so many. It's hard to pick one. But the biggest aspect that I would like to think that my players or the players that I've coached would experience after they leave the sport is self-confidence.

How can sports help athletes in school?

When you're a young person, you're looking for an identity. I think that middle school and high school gives a young person an opportunity to be a part of something and to feel self-worth and they're developing an identity of who they are. It might not be who they always are, but it does give them direction.

Sports allow you an opportunity to learn self-discipline, along with the discipline of schoolwork and academics.

As you grow into a college athlete, it becomes even more important that you have an ability to discipline your own self because there's so much freedom once you get into college. Do you go to the gym on your own time? Do you study on your own time? What do you do with your free time? So much of that is self-discipline, so I think if they learned that at a young age, to have a structure about the way they discipline themselves, then it carries over into their experience as student athletes in college.

What is your one piece of advice to an athlete that would help them think beyond being just an athlete?

One of the things that is really, really important to me is that they figure out what their passion is. I think that when they first come to college, they all think their passion is basketball. Obviously, it has to be a part of who they are or they wouldn't be here. I think what's interesting is to watch them grow as women and figure out that they can actually be a leader in the community, or they could actually own their own business, or be whoever they want to be. They can figure out what it is that they are really passionate about outside of sports.

My biggest responsibility is to make sure that when they leave here they are prepared for that next job interview. The one where they know they can beat out that person for that interview, and they have all the confidence in the world that they can do whatever job is put in front of them. They can face whatever adversity comes with that job or with life. I've always thought that if they leave here and they're not a little more prepared for that, then we haven't done a very good job of coaching, if all we're worried about is whether we win or lose.

My best advice would be to get outside of your bubble. It would be to not just network with other student athletes or just your teammates. It would be to get to know your professors. That would be my biggest advice, for them to see that they have the world in front of them. If you're a college athlete, someday it will be about something bigger than sports. I think that a lot of them just don't take advantage of that opportunity.

Also, be organized. That would be another thing. Be proactive, and there's a lot that goes into that. But I think what I mean by that is don't wait until you walk across the stage to start thinking about your plan. To be proactive is to start planning your junior year, not spring of your senior year. So proactive, to me, is really, really important, and it's really hard for them to do because they live where everything's in the moment. And network.

What do you believe are three key traits that athletes pick up from sports?

Discipline and structure; I think those two go hand-in-hand, and teamwork.

What do you think is an advantage that student athletes have over students who do not participate in sports?

Oh, I think that just goes back to the same thing. There's a certain self-confidence that comes from being in sports. I hate to say that it's just sports, because I think that extracurricular activities are really important. That's why I think finding your passion is important. Because being a part of something, whether it be that you're in the band or whether you're in Spanish club, I think grabbing onto something where you can be a part, and it's not just about you individually, is really, really important as you begin to grow.

I think sports is just a piece of that. It's a piece of a young person learning to thrive in a competitive environment, which is what the job world is like, and being able to be a part of a team, yet have individual goals, too. I think that's what's really neat about sports is that each player on my team has individual goals, and then they have team goals.

It's a process to learn how to achieve individual goals because they are important. But how do you put those in the framework of what our team goals are? I think that's an interesting dynamic that carries over into life. I mean, if you're a mother and a wife, then there are a lot of things that have to go into that. You can't just be about you and what you want to wake up and do every day. So, I think sports is an avenue of learning a lot of life lessons.

Why do you enjoy coaching your athletes and helping to keep them involved in sports?

One of the reasons why I chose to be a coach is because sports influenced me as a high school athlete. I was successful. Our team was successful. When I chose to coach, so much of it was that I wanted to show a young person what it felt like to be on a team and have a common goal. One of my biggest motivations to coach was that I think being on a team is selfless. I think that you learn there is something bigger than you when you're on a real team. So that's really one of the main reasons that I coach.

I think the other reason why I enjoy the experience of coaching is that eventually a kid will realize that they actually can do things that they didn't know they were capable of. They don't know it in the moment, but I think that sports teach you that you actually are capable of pushing yourself to a limit that you didn't know you were capable of. That's one of my biggest enjoyments is to see someone that maybe at the beginning didn't think they could do something, and then they all of a sudden become successful at whatever it is. It might be that sport, or it might be whatever they chose to do in education and you see them start to overcome.

What does "using sports as a vehicle" mean to you?

Sports is just an avenue of building your resume of who you are. It's a path that leads you to who you are and who you want to be. I think that the biggest thing is that it is just a path, and it's not the end-all.

So many young people think that sports are going to last forever. It is a vehicle for you to network with other people. It's a vehicle to get an education. It's a path. It's a road to an education. It can be a road to a job. I think education is power, and to me, sports can be that vehicle for an education.

Chapter 13

INTERVIEW WITH AN ATHLETE & RETIRED COACH

JILL STERKEL

JILL STERKEL

STATS

➤ 4x U.S. Olympic swim team member; two gold medals and two bronze medals.

➤ Honda Cup Award Winner

➤ Outstanding Female Collegiate Athlete

➤ NCAA Titles; won 16 out of 20 and was second in three.

➤ World Championship U.S. Water Polo Team

➤ The University of Texas Associate Athletic Director of the T Association

➤ The University of Texas Assistant and Head Coach; 1986 - 2005

INTERVIEW

What do you believe are at least three benefits of playing sports?

One of the biggest benefits is that you learn personal accountability. In other words, the work that you put in, is what you get out, most of the time. I would say it teaches you how to set small goals to get to the next steps, and then using that feedback to keep moving forward. Time management and the value of hard work are other benefits. And it gives you a personal satisfaction of accomplishment.

What are some ways that you believe coaches, high school counselors, or maybe even academic people in a college role, serve athletes?

I think it is just being there. As an athlete, I didn't see it, even though I felt it. As a coach, it brought to mind the words that a coach says, the words that anyone who is mentoring kids, young athletes or young people say. People remember those words. People remember your influence on them and how powerful that can be in a positive or a negative way.

Growing up as a young athlete, I definitely admired certain coaches, certain people. And they had an effect on my life in terms of my overall growth and development. So, understanding that, it's not a heavy burden, or a burden at all. But it is a huge responsibility that all educators in any area have. You can make a huge impact on somebody's life and change the trajectory of where they're going. And that is super powerful. It could be a positive or a negative experience. Obviously, we want the positive. It is critical to understand the power that your words and your actions have and the effect on other people.

__What is one thing you wish athletes would do to help prepare them-__
__selves beyond being just an athlete?__

I would like them to understand that each day is precious. Once you live this day, it's done; you don't have very many of them to hone your craft. Time will run out. I think that's hard for people to understand when they're only looking at what's ahead of them. It's easy when you've done it and you think, "Ah, I should have done this." It is important for them to prepare for life without a sport, and consider who they are without the sport. Really investing in themselves, finding their identity, and taking the time to do that. A lot of times, especially in a high-powered collegiate setting, you're focusing on your work and trying to make it through. A lot of your focus and mental preparation is in your sport. You have to pull some of that over and use it in other areas. That's hard to do because there's only so many hours in a day, but I think it's important.

I would also encourage them to live their life to their fullest in their sport. But always work on where you're going to end up. Let's say you're a great basketball player and your goal is to go to college; that's great. But what do you want to do beyond that? They should challenge themselves to work on that other side of their person. They are not going to be whole unless they do that. Don't be afraid to work on it. It is important to have good mentors, other people, parents, guiding you and pushing you along the way so that you do not let that other side sort of disappear. Those who do this will be much better off down the line if they stay open to doing this.

How can sports help athletes in school?

I think all those benefits definitely apply. It really teaches you. There's no hiding, and you can't fake it. You typically, for the most part, are putting deposits into a bank and then you're hoping to cash them out at the end of the season in terms of performances or whatever. Again, sometimes it's not immediate, but you get feedback about the work that you put in by your performance. And learning from the times when you fail, and then learning from the times you succeed and taking all that information and helping you be a better person, be a better athlete, survive in life at a higher level. It kept me out of trouble, for sure. I was busy doing my sport and so I didn't have idle time to just hang out with my friends. Not that I would have gotten in trouble, but the likelihood of me getting in trouble would have been higher.

Self-esteem comes from playing sports. There's all the statistics for women in terms of leadership skills, parlaying them into the workforce based on playing sport as a young athlete or as a collegiate athlete. The pregnancy statistics drop significantly. Staying in school, even just high school, all those statistics are affected in a positive way for those people who are involved in sports. These are valuable statistics, but just for the general health and well-being of somebody, sports are a huge plus.

What are some areas that you see athletes struggle with?

I think a lot of times they don't understand the skills that they've honed in their sport or from being on a team or being involved. They have this toolbox and I don't think they understand all the tools that they have. When I went from coaching to administration, I remember saying, "Well I've never done this before. I don't know how to do this." One of my friends said, "You're kidding me, you were coaching people using all those same tools."

Your work ethic and your skill set parlays. It just parlays in a different way. It's like learning how to pivot or take that turn and use the skills that you had only in a different arena. They still apply; they always are going to apply. Sometimes, we need to give a little instruction manual with that toolbox. Or connect the dots so that people see how they correlate and how they can use them and be more self-confident. Once an athlete gets in a situation in a work environment and then they get it, all that stuff comes out. But it would be nice to have that in the interview.

What do you believe are three key traits that athletes pick up from sports?

I would say accountability. What you put in it, you will get out of it. That's feedback and there's no hiding. Another is tenacity. Be willing to come back, day after day after day after day. Always work on improving to get better. I think that in terms of working with others, being a team player. Even in swimming, that's kind of an individual sport, but at the college level, it's very much a team sport. So, really learning how to be a good teammate. I think that's a huge benefit skill that you learn. I would say, the value of being on time. Practice starts at this time, you show up and you're on time. That's a learned trait over time.

What are some advantages you believe athletes have over kids who do not play sports?

In addition to the other things I have said, I have found in my college experience, it's people working for a common goal, to accomplish something, and to go through all the ups and downs and everything that you do. And all the life lessons that you learn, it's like in a family. You can't put a price tag on that. To me, it's almost like getting that stamp of approval. The experience of working together as a team over a period of time, trying to reach for the highest pinnacle, I think that's a pretty special experience.

In what ways do you feel sports have contributed to athletes' success? So when you think of people in a work field, how do you feel or think that sports helped with that?

I think it helps them be more resilient. Work, like anything, is day in and day out. I think you're more equipped to handle failures. I think you're more equipped to handle the successes. I think you're more equipped to just keep coming back and brushing yourself off and getting back up again.

Those are all the things that you learn through sports. Nobody's sporting life is perfect. You're learning from everything that you're doing. And work is no different. You're in a job and there's going to be great days and bad days. But if you've been through those years of Division 1 collegiate, you've got that stamp of approval. You've been through hard experiences, you know what to expect, and you know it's not going to kill you. And you come in and you keep pressing on.

What does "using sports as a vehicle" mean to you?

For me, it totally meant an opportunity to get an education at a great institution. I grew up in Southern California. My parents were middle class, and it probably wouldn't have been an option for me to come to The University of Texas if I had to pay for myself to come here. So, sports for me, in the State of California, it opened my eyes to the different colleges there. It was like, wow, I can maybe go to UCLA, USC, Stanford, places like that. Or now, I can look at Florida, I can look at Texas, I can look at these different places. It just opened doors for me that I wouldn't have had otherwise. And so, for me it was a vehicle to get an amazing education.

CONCLUSION

Let's be honest. The ball has to stop bouncing one day. There will not be any more touchdowns, there will not be any more homeruns or three pointers made. Your touchdown will now be you landing a job. That three-pointer made will now be you accomplishing one of your goals that you set for yourself. The excitement you got from that homerun will now be the excitement you get from watching your kids achieve their goals.

At a very young age, I had a dream to play professional basketball in the WNBA and I wanted to be just like Sheryl Swoopes. I thought I was the female version of Allen Iverson. Yes, I had the wristbands and headbands and wore both of their numbers. At some point, all athletes, including myself, thought sports would be all we did or would be the only way to make a lot of money.

To put things in perspective, there are 60 picks in the NBA draft and 36 picks in the WNBA draft with over 15,000 athletes participating in each. Only .09 percent of athletes continue on to play in the WNBA and only 1.2 percent for the NBA. Football drafts 253 athletes, with a percentage of only 1.6 percent of athletes playing in the NFL. Looking at these numbers, there may be a select few who have the opportunity to play professional sports after college. However, according to the NFL Players Association, the average career length in the NFL is three and one third years, while it is five years for the NBA. Of course, there are athletes who play longer, but on average, five years is the max.

The question you must ask yourself is, "What will I do when it's over?" How will you use all the blood, sweat and tears poured into your sport? As you have read throughout this book, sports can teach you many things about yourself and allow you to pick up lots of good habits.

The key is to translate that to your personal life, whether that is your career field, your relationships or your day-to-day operations. If you are able to still look at whatever you are doing as if it was your sport, you can dominate anything you do! That is how you approached each game and each opponent, right? You have to look at yourself through a more complete lens, because, after all, if you are not playing professionally, then you are not an athlete anymore.

Once you finish your sport, you now become a FORMER athlete. For example, I am Ashley Roberts who is an entrepreneur that played basketball at The University of Texas. Entrepreneurship is my identity and anything else that I do business related. Although people know me through playing sports, it does not define who I am and aspire to be.

The problem with most athletes is that we stop at being just a former athlete without having a new identity. This new identity should be the starting point and not the ending point. Whether you are looking into entrepreneurship or being the next doctor, you should be able to use all of what your sport taught you and what being an athlete represented.

As an athlete, you were always held to a higher standard and were expected to do things differently than non-athletes. The same thing should apply. As athletes, we competed every day against our teammates, as well as in games against opponents. The goal was to win. The same thing applies in life. Playing sports allows you to have a different mindset than non-athletes. Tailoring that mindset is a key factor in your success for life after sports.

It is never too early to start thinking about your lane after sports. It also is never too late. However, you do not want to be the one who is stuck not knowing what to do once sports is over. You cannot play sports forever, which means it will stop one day. Will you be prepared for the next chapter? Will you be ready to step into your new lane? I want you to think about how long you have been playing sports. I know for me, it was over 18 years. That is how long some people have been on their job or been married. Out of those 18 years on the job, I was able to learn a ton of things that have helped me outside of sports. I mean, 18 years is a long time to just let everything go to waste.

Some of those things included time management, handling situations under pressure, finding a way to get things done, no matter the situation, being a team player, to name just a few. If you are not learning anything but just playing the sport, thinking the pros is your ticket, then you have it all wrong.

Whether you have been playing sports for one year or twenty years, it is imperative that each year, each month, each day, you are learning something that is going to benefit you as a person, your life and your future. Basketball not only allowed me to take away valuable information, but also shaped who I am as a person. It helped me find my identity and see different things in myself that I don't think I would have found without sports.

Another piece of advice is to make friends with your teammates! You are with them pretty much all day, everyday. Your teammates will become your life-long friends; and even friends you can call sisters or brothers. As you grow older, those teammates will start to find their passion and what they like to do and it will be even more rewarding when you guys are there to share those moments. Being able to be in special events, such as weddings, baby showers, etc., is a benefit of being in a team sport that allows you to connect with many different people.

Playing sports allowed me to get a free education and leverage it for my profession as an entrepreneur. As you already read, my entrepreneurship journey started as a third grader. Selling candy was a part of my life until high school. Cheddar's was another job I had during high school. I was being taught at an early age what work felt like, and I enjoyed the process of making and having my own money. I bought my very first car myself with the money I was making from my job. I was learning how to manage work, school and sports, all at the same time.

I had to make many sacrifices, in that I couldn't always hang out with my friends or go to all the football games. I was learning how to communicate with others at my job by giving them the correct orders. I was preparing myself for the real world and I was also gaining an understanding of how teamwork works. I was able to learn in more depth all of these same things within the game of basketball.

Basketball was not who I was, but what I did. I am Ashley Roberts and I am the owner of Competitive Edge, LLC. Within Competitive Edge, I have a basketball company that hosts camps, clinics, basketball teams and runs events with much more in store. I am also proud to say that I am a first-time author!

You have read this book and gained some insight on how to leverage sports. Let me ask you, who are you? Really, who are you? After answering the questions from Its In Your Court, take some time to jot down in the Notes section who you are and what you enjoy doing besides sports.

Look at those things and piece them together to find out what you can see yourself doing. How will you define yourself once the game ends? Speak it into existence. Write it down in the Notes section three times and say it out loud each time. I WILL BE A DOCTOR or I WILL BE A TEACHER or I WILL BE AN ENTREPRENEUR. Whatever it is write it out and believe it!

IT'S IN
YOUR COURT

➤ What are some takeaways you got from *Changing Lanes*?

_____

_____

_____

_____

➤ List three things you are going to apply to your life?

_____

_____

_____

_____

➤ Which chapter stood out to you the most? Go back and read it again.

_____

_____

_____

_____

➤ Share this book with a friend and post on your social media. Be sure to tag me in it!

_____

_____

_____

_____

Notes

Notes

ABOUT THE AUTHOR

Ashley Roberts is a native of Dallas, Texas and a former women's basketball letter winner at The University of Texas. While on the 40 acres, Roberts received her bachelor's degree in Physical Culture and Sports with a minor in Business. Currently, Roberts is furthering her education in pursuit of a master's degree from her alma mater.

Under the guidance of former coaches, Roberts was exposed to a form of leadership that enables her to excel on the court and rise to the forefront as a young female coach. Roberts has had the pleasure of coaching young ladies on various levels from elementary to high school. She prides herself on teaching these young ladies how to utilize sports as a vehicle to drive them through life instead of just perfecting the skill set of their sport.

Coach Roberts wants to spread the knowledge that has attributed to her success in the coaching industry. Her expertise, passion, and drive has fueled her in creating a system that empowers those who aspire to achieve success at the next level. With the proper guidance and mentorship, Roberts believes that she can help players develop as they grow as individuals on and off the court.

For additional information about Ashley Roberts, please contact her at the following:

 www.ashleynroberts.com

 _thisisashleyr

 _thisisashleyr

 info@ashleynroberts.com

Made in the USA
Middletown, DE
17 July 2020